Praise for

UnWasteD

"A gripping, inspiring tale that picks up where most sobriety memoirs leave off, at the beginning of a harrowing journey through commitment and tenacity. This is a story for anyone trying to enact meaningful change in their lives of any kind."
—Emma McLaughlin and Nicola Kraus,
co-authors of *The Nanny Diaries*

"Sacha Z. Scoblic's often funny, always honest, and wholly unflinching look at her sobriety is not to be missed. As Sacha chooses her life, you'll choose this author: she's a revelation."
—Megan Crane, author of *I Love the 80s* and
Names My Sisters Call Me

"With lucid, elegant prose, Sacha paints a painfully accurate picture of sobriety. Entertaining and enlightening, her writing is a companion for those who have given up the bottle and a brilliant illustration for those who live anywhere near addiction."
—Therese Borchard, author of *Beyond Blue*

"As someone who's been drunk with Sacha Scoblic, I can attest that she's even smarter, sweeter and funnier when sober. This book is all of those things, one of the best memoirs I've read in a long time, and a compelling answer to anyone wondering what life is like on the other side of alcoholism."
—Tucker Carlson

"Unwasted takes us on the mind trip that early recovery tends to be; Scoblic's vivid depiction of the ultimate perseverance of finding a new and fulfilling life will surely motivate."
—Jennifer Storm, author of *Blackout Girl* and
Leave the Light On

UnWasted

My Lush Sobriety

Sacha Z. Scoblic

CITADEL PRESS
Kensington Publishing Corp.
www.kensingtonbooks.com

CITADEL PRESS BOOKS are published by

Kensington Publishing Corp.
119 West 40th Street
New York, NY 10018

Some of the material in *Unwasted* is based on columns written for
The New York Times

All Kensington titles, imprints, and distributed lines are available at
special quantity discounts for bulk purchases for sales promotions,
premiums, fund-raising, educational, or institutional use. Special book
excerpts or customized printings can also be created to fit specific needs.
For details, write or phone the office of the Kensington special sales
manager: Kensington Publishing Corp., 119 West 40th Street, New York,
NY 10018, attn: Special Sales Department; phone 1-800-221-2647.

CITADEL PRESS and the Citadel logo are Reg. U.S. Pat. & TM Off.

First printing: August 2011

10 9 8 7 6 5 4

Printed in the United States of America

CIP data is available.

ISBN-13: 978-0-8065-3429-9
ISBN-10: 0-8065-3429-X

For Peter, who pulls the demons out of my ears. Always.
And for my father, who led the way.

Contents

Contents

Author's Note

Many names and identifying characteristics have been changed throughout this book to protect the privacy of persons involved.

UnWasted

UNWASTED

Introduction

Reality is a hallucination brought on by lack of alcohol.

—Anonymous

I wasn't a teenage runaway. I wasn't a counterculture icon. I didn't beat up a cop while high and spend three months in the clink. I'm just an average chick living in the city—Okay, in Washington, D.C.—who used to get wasted. Every night.

But this book isn't about my wasted life. It's about what happened when I put down the bottle, when I got unwasted.

My first year clean, I found myself constantly confounded and mocked by time itself, embraced by those who were formerly the object of my envy (and ire), surrounded by new social protocols, and plagued by outlandish and uncontrollable relapse fantasies. Sometimes, between the craziness of a hazy past drenched in booze and an odd present teeming with vivid hues and clarity, my imagination went into overdrive. Cleaving my life in two—before and after—did not mean I had lost my desire to swim in alcoholic waters. And,

1

in early sobriety, I could still see the liquor lapping at my feet, beseeching me to take one last dip. The thought of relapsing came hard and quick early on—from banal longings for a sip of wine after work to elaborately constructed sophistries designed to free my conscience from the guilt of backsliding and to ignore the Herculean effort of getting sober to begin with. And so, staggered throughout this book are these fantasy relapses, all of the unfulfilled wishful drinking I just couldn't shake—at first. Because something funny happened to me after a couple of years of sobriety: The life I had was better than any fantasy.

In other words, sobriety has turned out to be its own adventure. And, nowadays, I want to live a big life, where every moment goes unwasted.

Chapter 1

Rock Star, Meet Teetotaler

The little tables in the restaurant shimmered under the moody lighting—just the kind of lighting that after a few drinks would take on a shadowy glow and make your table the only table, a tiny oasis. But it was autumn and here I was: three months stone-cold sober, out of the house for the first time in weeks, and meeting new people—an intimidatingly attractive couple, Hanna and Evan, with bright smiles and even brighter careers. I wanted to hate them, to cede ground on the looks and success fronts but retain intellectual superiority. It was a lost cause; they were so damn funny right away that I couldn't help but be disarmed. Hanna was especially arch as she told wicked stories about life as a divorce attorney ("You have to mourn it like a death," she deadpanned to an invisible client). I was smitten. Her eyes were mischievous when she leaned over to me and asked, "Shall we order a bottle of wine?" It was as though she was letting me in on a secret, a little bit of whimsy that she wanted to share with me, her table sister, while our wonky mates talked foreign policy.

"No thanks, I don't drink," I said apologetically, certain I had just irrevocably denounced the possibility of a good time that night, rebuffed her sweet attempt at inclusion, and declared myself a Mormon all in one fell swoop. Which is perhaps why my next words—rushing out of my mouth with a kind of desperate lunacy—were: "But don't worry, I'm still fun!" Like that was normal. Like that didn't sound anything at all like a pert promise-ring girl trying to assure her frustrated, panting boyfriend that we could do lots of things besides have sex. Because, really, how fun could I possibly be if I didn't drink?

I was acutely aware of my own feeling toward people who didn't drink, which was that they were obviously vanilla, uptight squares who secretly wanted me to treat my body like a temple, take Jesus Christ as my savior, and drink Kool-Aid with them at mixers in church basements. Or they were health nuts who got "high" by hiking Mount Kilimanjaro or taking six-hour heated power yoga sessions while communing with their inner gurus or doing other activities that smacked of effort. But the worst thing was that I feared even those folks were more interesting—if exasperatingly earnest—than I was sober.

Drinking had given me an alter ego par excellence. I was

the rock star at every party, nightclub, and living room I wafted into, happily singing or dancing like life was meant only for such pursuits. I was ready to see any evening through until dawn, to wear sequins and glitter if necessary, and to laugh until black eyeliner ran down my face. My favorite word was "subversive," and my favorite humor was cruel. Every day was hard, but every night was Saturday night. Once, as a boyfriend implored me to take it easy, to call it a night, I looked to the friends waiting for me on the sidewalk ready to go to the next party and replied, "But this is who I am. I'm a fun girl."

And, for a long time, I was fun. Or at least I was having fun. In my twenties, along with my friends Jack and Tessa, I stepped into an alternate universe in Washington, D.C.—a kind of Neverland, where Jack, Tessa, and I cocooned into one another, where every joke was an inside joke, where every night was ours for the taking.

In winter, I would slip from my apartment in D.C.'s Adams Morgan neighborhood in nothing but flannel pajamas and dash through a cold night to Tessa's house around the corner; she would be waiting with hot toddies and cigarettes, and we would build a fort on the floor and watch old, scary cult movies like *Freaks, Carnival of Souls,* or *The Wicker Man* until we passed out.

In the spring, we'd take Ecstasy and go to gay clubs with Jack. Tessa would sit on the clubs' huge speakers like a tiny punk-rock Buddha while Jack and I would dance and laugh. Eventually we would all huddle together and jump up and down in sync with the beat to our favorite nightclub song: "Unspeakable Joy!" Then we would wander home like ghosts, lowering all the blinds while Tessa meticulously turned all the clocks around or covered them with sweaters. And I would try to remember that I hadn't done anything wrong, that it was okay to stay up all night, that I was an adult. But somewhere I felt red flags flashing in the back of my mind, and I poured myself another drink.

In summer, the three of us would order margaritas on the patio of every bar in the neighborhood and people-watch. Invariably Jack and I would wrestle, Tessa would push me down the street in an empty shopping cart, or we would all fall down laughing. I would wake up so bruised, I'd have to wear jeans all of August. One day, when Jack and I went to the pool at a nearby hotel (Tessa eschewed the sun and wore a giant rice-paddy hat all summer), I looked as though I had been beaten to within an inch of my life. "I don't know why you stay with him," Jack would yell as loud as he could as I walked to the edge of the pool. "He shouldn't treat you like that!" I'd fall into the pool screaming with laughter while the hotel guests looked on with horror.

In the autumn, the three of us would carve pumpkins and drink beer on the stoop, and Jack would laugh at me for puking all over Tessa's couch the night before. I would start to feel the stress of another Sunday coming to a close, of another season coming to a close, of another year coming to a close. How long would I stay like this? How long until it was ridiculous that I hadn't started my life yet? Should I have a drink right now?

It was the late 90s, and none of us were finding the same kind of love outside of our triumvirate as we had within it. And it wasn't long before I began to feel stagnant, like my life was on hold. As hilarious and special as any given moment with my two best friends often was, those moments were always an escape from what was really going on with me. And what was really going on wasn't so sexy and exciting: I suffered from crippling panic attacks every day in the predawn and early morning hours, my financial situation was a catastrophe, I had dropped out of law school and I found myself uncertain of how to create the life I wanted—or what that life might even look like. I just knew in my bones that temp jobs and partying weren't all I was meant to do with this ride.

So I made some changes. I earned a graduate degree in journalism and landed a proper job. I began operating under this whole work-hard/play-hard philosophy I developed that involved hurtling through life at breakneck speed and saying *Yes!* to everything. Would I like to write articles for cookies instead of money for a new start-up website? Yes! Would I like to try the mushrooms my roommate's sister's boyfriend grew from scratch? Yes! The tension within me was explosive. I loved being the rock star, but it stopped being enough. Some potent little glowing force inside me paid enough attention to graduate school, to jobs, to normal life, that in the new millennium I wound end up working at a magazine where the contradictions in my world revealed themselves more nakedly. At the time, I assumed either cosmic intervention or a gas leak in the building had led to me getting hired at *The New Republic* magazine. Still, I was completely ready to emulate Hunter S. Thompson: I'd drink all night and write colorful scene-scapes about American zeitgeist by day. I'd churn out material people would still be reading thirty years from now, my own fear and loathing on the campaign trail. I had elevated "high-functioning alcoholic" to an art form. Unfortunately, at *The New Republic*, even the interns, some of whom were Rhodes Scholars, scared the shit out of me:

Intern: Did you see the House vote on C-SPAN last night?

Me: Um . . . (*No way, loser, I was too busy playing the board game Mystery Date with Tessa and drinking vodka-Diet Pepsis.*)

And that was just the interns. At editorial meetings, I'd sit frozen and terrified while one editor quoted Maimonides and another broke down the finer points of privatizing Social Security.

My first month into the job at *The New Republic*, the staff went out for a happy hour. I threw back drinks and encouraged my new colleagues to join me for shots. When that request was a bust, I called Jack from outside the bathroom. "They're all so shiny and normal," I whispered. "I think some of them may never have smoked pot!" Exactly half of me wanted to thrill and shock the *New Republic* crowd with stories of my exploits as a much cooler and darker person than my façade let on. And exactly half of me was certain I would be found out for what I really was: not up to snuff, proud of the wrong things, and terrified all the time. I was divided against myself.

One night, a *New Republic* happy hour turned particularly loose, and it seemed everyone was drinking at my pace. Somehow I became engaged in a conversation with a sharp political writer named Eddie as to which one of us was wilder. It was the dumb kind of thing one can only discuss when totally blitzed because it would be too inane a topic for anyone with a shred of self-awareness to even broach. I respected Eddie and, worse, liked him; but, at a magazine where I felt like a loser a lot of the time, I smelled a solid win. One more shot of bourbon gave my competitiveness an edge over my discretion, and I heard myself say, "Well, let's just lay it on the table. How many drugs have you done?" I had been challenged and I was ready to go story-for-story with Eddie. For every rich-kid, coke-fueled, penthouse-apartment romp I cruelly imagined Eddie tossing at me, I'd parry with a crystal-meth binge in the back of a gay club while a purple Teletubby walked by. Because "wild" was my wheelhouse, bitch, and this rock star was ready to play. In retrospect, I can see that perhaps Eddie and I had different definitions of "wild" or that perhaps Eddie was every bit as twisted as myself (after all, why should I be the only night-crawling vampire at *The New Republic*?). Luckily for all present and especially me, Eddie wisely walked away from the conversation. *Ha! Gotcha!* I thought triumphantly. And yet, even as I basked in my self-perceived victory, I sensed something broken deep inside of me.

It's a moment that has haunted me for years. That moment I realized I was growing uncomfortable with the role of Wild Chick, that being "most wild" was not a title I truly wanted, that I was playing a game without winners. If the only superlative I could claim in this crowd was "wildest," I was sure to end up deeply unhappy. Because, if the staff at *The New Republic* seemed somehow innocent, they were also incredibly successful in all the best ways: toiling in a world of ideas; writing contemporary America into being; marrying clever, witty people; and sparring in a kind of verbal speed symphony that made my college debate team sound like fishmongers. They were razor-sharp and wry, and while they weren't necessarily edgy, they were still a lot of fun to be around; in fact, I could have as much fun around the lunch table at *The New Republic* as I could in an evening out with Tessa and Jack. For reasons I couldn't fathom, I felt right at home.

I worked at *The New Republic* for years under the work-hard/play-hard philosophy. And before I left to take a job at *Reader's Digest*, I was reminded of that terrible competitive moment with Eddie. While toasting me good-bye, my *New Republic* editor asked aloud, "Where did we find Sacha anyway?" A voice in the crowd was quick with the answer: "At a bar!" We all laughed, and everyone looked at me lovingly, their wacky Sacha. But, inside, I winced. I knew the sentiment was a direct hit even if I would not yet admit to it out loud. You don't make fun of the drinking habits of actual addicts; so my colleagues didn't yet know how close to the truth they were. But I must have, because I winced. I knew that, behind the black shrouds of denial I wrapped myself in, I was nothing more than a drunk who charmed these clever intellectuals into letting her hang out for a while. I had been jester in their court for years. Indeed, the last time I'd attended a going-away party for a colleague, I'd ended the evening by throwing up outside the historic and expertly groomed Hay-Adams Hotel in the shadow of the White House. More and more, my good-time lifestyle conflicted with the professional and personal life I was trying to create.

Unsurprisingly, the rock-star life came with a dark side. One does not emulate Hunter S. Thompson and then go skipping through the lilies with nary a consequence. I'd had a few scares, a few terrifying nights that should have set me straight immediately. A couple years earlier, for example, I had met an old grad school friend, Scott, at a bar. But, when I wasn't content to go home at closing time—*because, my friends, there is more drinking to be done!*—I ended up at a seedy strip club with Scott and his friend Andy. The strip club was all that was open at that hour, I reasoned. So I sat and drank vodka-tonics while pretending that the whole occasion was not uncomfortable at all, but rather an opportunity to express my devotion to feminism and my enlightened stand on sexual politics. Instead of acting on my own actual principles or, for that matter, even bothering to have any principles (like, say, self-respect, care, and protection), I simply chiseled my morals down to fit the situation. As twentysomething girls looking more prepubescent than womanly strolled by in a kind of morose slow-motion, I buried my own doubts about the night in vodka.

When Andy suggested we drive to his cocaine dealer's for a nightcap, I jumped into his SUV. I was enjoying being the girl who was up for anything, scared of nothing, willing to let the night take her where it may. I was so intoxicated by my own idea of myself in that moment that no other thoughts could make it to the surface of my brain. And though Scott parted ways with us there, I instinctively trusted Andy, a complete stranger, to see me through the night. After all, he had seemed completely unfazed when I calmly explained that I would not be going to bed with him; I just wanted to go to the next party, event, or after-hours and have some fun. I wanted to go exploring. But, when Andy pulled over to the side of the road in an unfamiliar neighborhood to pick up a prostitute, I realized I had made a big mistake. Trapped between my free-wheeling persona for that night, who thought it might be interesting to discuss objectification versus em-powerment with this woman, and some intense internal part of myself begging to be released from the boozy fortifications within, I felt paralyzed. That is when I finally woke up to the fact that the evening had gone too far—not in the strip club surrounded by vile men and laconic women, not when Scott left, not when a trip to a coke dealer was on the table, but, finally, in the SUV as a bedraggled woman of the night climbed in behind me and directed Andy to a house where he could score drugs. It was only then that it even occurred to me that I had long before crossed a line I should never have crossed. I missed Jack and Tessa intensely. For every bad decision we had ever made, for every rock-star night we'd ever taken by storm, I always felt that Jack in particular was looking out for me, guiding my decisions. Tessa even called him our "cruise director."

Feeling completely alone now in the SUV with my own catastrophic choices, I asked to be driven home. Andy po-litely told me I could call a taxi from "the house." I dared not argue with him as I could now more clearly see a sense of mission spreading across his face. Somehow I was no longer a fun companion; I was utterly disposable and irrelevant. We pulled up to a small one-story house not far from the city, where a man and a woman who were clearly used to guests at all hours casually let us in. There was drug para-phernalia strewn across the kitchen table—pipes, needles, plastic baggies—and I suddenly felt very naïve. *I just wanted to keep drinking; I didn't really want this.* Andy's prostitute asked me if it was okay if she took him to another room in what I can only assume was a kind of warped but oddly disarming moment of female loyalty. "He's all yours," I said quietly, barely grasping her meaning. Meanwhile, the man and woman who had let us in offered me a cornucopia of illicit options. But, before I could answer, I heard a small child cough from a room behind me. "My son," said the woman. "He has asthma." And that soft noise, the child's cough, a kind of delicate hurt, brought reality rushing in. I started to cry. "I've made a mistake," I told them. "I have to go home." And without getting the address or calling a cab, I walked through the front door into the unfamiliar street and headed for what looked to be a main thoroughfare. I felt my legs go quickly, until I was running. Were they coming after me? I now knew where their drug house was! And all I could think to do was to get as much distance between me and the house and the coughing child as possible.

What happened next is what my friends in twelve-step programs would call "not a coincidence"—the kind of stars-aligning moment that many addicts would have seen as a sign: A taxi pulled up to a light just as I ran up to it and the driver still took me home even after I admitted I only had five dollars on me—a mere third of the eventual fare. I was in my own apartment twenty minutes later, hugging my knees and marveling at the perfect timing of my escape chariot. Jack yelled at me for a long time on the phone the next morning as I relayed the nightmare ("I let you out of my sight for one night and you end up at a crack house?!"). And, for the first time, I deeply considered giving up drinking and starting a new way of life. But the stars did not align, and the thought did not last longer than a few days. I had managed to create a good career and forge my way in the world; it stood to reason that I could control my alcohol consumption. And, five years after that sad night running from a drug den in the cold, I felt like a court jester among my savvy journalist friends. That was the second time I seriously thought about changing my life and leaving alcohol behind.

And for all of those years that I happily played editor at *The New Republic* and basked in the pleasure of Jack's and Tessa's irrepressible personalities, I also still lived with debilitating panic attacks, night terrors, and soul-sucking guilt. I whizzed through one antidepressant after another, even though I could never isolate why I felt so awful, why I was so consumed with pain. So I did what I always did and threw a little booze at the problem, and then a little more. Until I was drinking every night, enough so that I was able to pass out. Nothing scared me more than going to bed sober, alone with my head.

Friends from work and boyfriends throughout the years had long implored me to do something about my drinking. "My Drinking"—like it was an ill-behaved child I carried around everywhere. A little ugly gnome that popped its head out from behind me every now and then to utter inappropriate insults ("Did you see that dress? What a crack whore!") or wax on about its many and varied adventures and experiences in life from which you, Sacha's friend, should really learn (like "Everyone should try Ecstasy at least once in their life, because, dude, everyone should be that happy, you know?"). My Drinking was also unruly and apt to break wineglasses, tumblers, beloved antique crystal goblets, and any delicate *objets d'art* in My Drinking's path. My Drinking was also vulnerable to becoming ill at a moment's notice and spending an hour vomiting in your bathroom while you rolled your eyes and noted that My Drinking was not as fun as it used to be. And, of course, the more you came to know My Drinking, the more likely you were to find My Drinking sobbing uncontrollably at the end of the evening for reasons that were convoluted and at times utterly opaque. And I defended My Drinking to the hilt, as if it were a misbehaving but beloved child. Other people were so uptight about My Drinking, but that was just because they didn't know My Drinking the way I did. They didn't know that My Drinking was the light of my life or the first thing I thought about when I got home from work.

Still, for years, I tried to control my drinking. Because God knows stopping drinking altogether was not even remotely up for consideration. Right there was a pretty big clue that I had a problem that exceeded my grasp. But grasp at it I did! I tried limiting my consumption to beer and wine, then just wine, then just three glasses a night, then one glass of water for each glass of wine, then no drinking on week-nights, then writing down a log of my drinks in an evening, then drinking only as much as the person I was with was drinking, and then—*Oh, fuck it!*—I'd wind up drunk. No drug I had ever tried captivated me the way booze had. Alcohol was my drug of choice. I'd love to stop at two or three; I really would. In fact, I thought if I could just prevent myself from getting into a state of drunkenness then I would be fine. I foolishly thought that I only lost control once drunk and that all of my subsequent bad decisions—like going to a shady after-hours bar at 3 A.M. on a weeknight—were just a result of being intoxicated already.

And then one Sunday afternoon in June, I went to meet Tessa for a drink to celebrate her birthday. I told Peter, then my boyfriend and now my husband, that I would be home for *60 Minutes*—and at the time, I meant it. I wasn't home for *60 Minutes*. I walked out of a bar at 7:30 the next morning. Monday morning. Just in time to shower and go to work at *Reader's Digest*, America's family magazine. Somehow, afternoon drinks on the patio led to evening drinks at a bar, which led to nighttime drinks and dancing at a club, which led to after-hours drinks at another bar, which led to more drinks and a marathon billiards match. Which led to the sun—the fucking sun—blinding me (and not for the first time) as I wandered into the street with no memory of even entering the bar I had just walked out of.

As the sun hit me that Monday morning in June, my logic

unraveled. I thought about all the times I had told Peter and myself—and many others along the way—that I would control my drinking. The bad decision wasn't going to the wrong bar at the wrong time. The bad decision was picking up that first drink of the day. Because what was sadly clear to me now was that seven or eight times out of every ten nights of drinking, I lost control. I might have a drink one night with friends and be fine; or I might walk out of a bar at 7:30 A.M. And, despite consistently noble intentions, I had absolutely no idea when I took my first sip which kind of night it would be. I was, and I am, an alcoholic. Why this occurred to me one morning in June as the sun bleached my vision and not when I ran from the drug house or at any other time is simple: Until that moment in June, I had not yet grown tired enough of an unmanageable and unpredictable life. You haven't hit bottom until you stop digging. Bottom isn't skid row or the heartbreaking sound of a child coughing; bottom is just where you happen to be when you stop tunneling and start climbing. For me, it was on Columbia Road in Washington, D.C.'s Adams Morgan neighborhood on a beautiful and piercing June morning.

All of those games I played to control my drinking were moot. Once the first sip of alcohol registered, the jig was up. Little addicted synapses all over my brain demanded more— no matter how sober I was after just one sip. Here's a secret: Alcoholism isn't all *Leaving Las Vegas* or the slurring mothers of after-school specials and *Lifetime* movies. I used to think that I wouldn't be an alcoholic until I woke up with the shakes or couldn't physically go a day without booze. But those are just the very visible and longer-term effects of the addiction. In fact, I was in the midst of a long stretch of a self-imposed No Drinking On Weekdays program when I walked into that bar.

The truth is, I probably left college addicted to alcohol. I had the right genetic markers, the right amount of exposure, and the right, shall we say, exploratory nature. Hell, my first word was "bottle" (seriously). But it took me another decade of bars, raves, clubs, and parties before it stopped working for me, before the life I had was so unmanageable (and so at odds with the life I had envisioned for myself) that I was willing to make a change—however drastic.

What I really craved was serenity. When I walked out of the bar that Monday morning, I just wanted my head to be quiet. I wanted to stop feeling the panic and guilt that seemed to come harder and faster with each drink. I wanted an easier way of life. And so, later that day—when Peter looked at me as we stood on the street outside his office and asked, "So what are you going to do?"—I knew I'd had my last drink. "I'm an alcoholic," I sputtered before devolving into tears on the sidewalk. I felt like someone had just died; the harsh and solitary feeling flooding my veins was one of abject grief. How would I manage to go on without alcohol? I knew I wouldn't last long if I didn't tell people right away.

So, to make it official, to enshrine it, I e-mailed the people it would affect most, Jack and Tessa—certain I had just done something horrible and irrevocable to our friendship. I felt like I was abandoning them and in a way abandoning the *idea* of us. I was leaving Neverland and in so doing acknowledging that it had never been real. I felt cruel. And though Jack and Tessa immediately wrote back supportive and loving e-mails, our friendship would end up changing. Soon we were all living in different cities; Tessa moved to Baltimore and Jack to Boston. Neverland was a shimmering memory. Meanwhile, I felt all alone in a new brighter, crisper, lonelier D.C.

Now that I was dry, was I still the rock star? Was I still the chick who took any dare, who stayed up the latest, who laughed the longest? Being dry was like being a blank slate. I had no particular traits ascribed to me, no particular habits or likes and dislikes. Would I still like to dance if I wasn't drunk? Would I still be funny? How much of the me I had come to know over the last decade-plus was even real? Apart from the alcohol and drugs, who was Sacha innately? I didn't know who I was anymore—just who I used to be. And though I chose to be clean, though I may not have known who I was going to become, a discordant and primal wail came up from within me in early sobriety: *I used to be a fucking legend!* If only I could shed the dark side without losing the rock star.

And so, when I told Hanna, the wry divorce attorney, that I didn't drink as we sat down to dinner, I also felt compelled to blurt out, "Don't worry, I'm still fun!" even though what

I was really thinking was: *Don't even for a minute think I'm vanilla because the truth is I am so hard core I had to quit. I drank so much it was a matter of life and death. I'm like a rock star compared with you. In fact, maybe you should just refer to me as Sid Vicious from now on. You should look at me with a touch of fear and awe because I am such a badass you would quiver just to think about the amount of rotgut I've ingested over the years. So step off with your preconceived notions, okay?*

In fact, throughout my entire first year of sobriety, I would have liked to have had a sign to that effect. Maybe a skull-and-crossbones-like symbol just for us addicts, something with the right mix of menace and solidarity, something I could tattoo on my wrist like a gang member with 150-proof street cred. That way, instead of reassuring new acquaintances that I was fun, I could just silently shake my head when offered a drink, flash my tat, and look at my new friend with a kind of weathered mystery. What I had yet to learn was how little people cared about whether I drank or not—and how little I needed to concern myself with what people did think.

In the meantime, the dissonance between the rock star within screaming to be let out and the insecure woman pledging to be fun was alarming to me. I mean, I hadn't the faintest idea of how to have fun without drinking. I was still discovering all sorts of terrible new truths, like how parties without drinking were really just a lot of people standing in the same room, and how movies I once found funny were often riddled with stilted language and bad dirty jokes. The real world was a totally new animal. And without my booze-fueled sense of rock-star self, I had no clue as to who I was—or whether or not I was any fun. I had lost my swagger.

So at the restaurant table, when the words "But don't worry, I'm still fun!" rushed out of my mouth in a chirpy adolescent squawk faster than I could inhale them back into my lungs, I was feeling a touch vulnerable. But my new pal at the table, Hanna, with the impish grin, did the unthinkable; without pausing to consider the crazy fact of my sobriety, without even a nanosecond of hesitation, she winked—winked!—and said, "Oh, good!" She was thrilled, it seemed, that I was "still fun"; nothing pleased her more. She was just glad it was all working out for me. And as for my embarrassing state of teetotalism, well, it was clear that she couldn't care less.

It was a good ten minutes before I could rejoin the conversation. I sat back in my chair away from the halo of the white tablecloth and watched the restaurant in slow motion while diners passed the bread, bantered with the salty waitress, poked at the tortellini, and guffawed at tales of office high jinks. They were all really enjoying themselves. Apparently, no one else in the restaurant cared whether I drank or not either. This wasn't, after all, spring break in Cancun, where turning down a yard-long tube of crushed ice and battery acid was prudish. This was real life, where in a nice restaurant in Washington no one looked askance at a thirty-two-year-old woman without a drink. Certainly my companions didn't; they seemed more interested in what I brought to the table than whether I put a glass of wine on it.

So I bid a silent good-bye to the internal rock-star speech (adieu, Sid Vicious!), promised to stop defining myself by who I used to be, and scooted my chair closer to the table. It was time to make some friends.

Number 1 on the Sacha Fantasy Relapse Pass: Hunter S. Thompson

Lots of addicts in recovery worry that they might relapse if they hang out with old friends, if they lose their job, or if a loved one dies. I, on the other hand, worry I might relapse if an exciting opportunity to get wasted with a celebrity comes along.

Recently, a friend told me an amazing story. During the summer of 2004, she had been in Aspen, Colorado, when her pal's cell phone rang. The pal answered the phone, explained the situation to my friend, and said, "Are you in?" The next thing my friend knew, she was at a house known to many as Owl Farm. There, she and a small group of people clustered around a bald man with tinted glasses and a penchant for pills. It was Hunter

S. Thompson. And, while my friend and a few others smoked pot and drank wine, Thompson actually read to them—excerpts of his own work from original 1970s issues of Rolling Stone magazine. Several months after my friend met him, the great writer died. "Huh," I said. After composing myself—I wavered in a kind of stunned jealousy for a few moments—I became consumed with just one thought: Obviously, in that situation, I would have to relapse.

Clearly, I am a Thompson fan. Perhaps because his addictions and his prose were so entwined and so visceral. Perhaps because he was writing during a time in which I'd always wished I had come of age. And so, for several long days, I obsessed over what avenues I might have taken in life to put me in a position to meet Hunter S. Thompson and have him read to me from an original Rolling Stone magazine while at Owl Farm. I even realized that—ha!—the night in question was almost a year before I quit drugs and alcohol. As if the fantasy could now be guilt-free. As if now, should time travel suddenly exist and should I be able to become my friend for a night, I'd be good to go.

And I can imagine it so well! While Thompson tells me about the Vegas articles, he hands me some patented cocktail of substances; maybe I demur at first, but then he says, "Every now and then when your life gets complicated and the weasels start closing in, the only cure is *to load up on heinous chemicals—and then drive like a bastard from Hollywood to Las Vegas with the music at top volume and at least a pint of ether." And that's when I look the strange and great man dead in the eyes and say, "Right. So is it okay if I mix the red pills with the purple ones?"*

More and more, it began to seem prudent to plan for such an evening, not of time travel and body-swapping, but of not-to-be-missed relapse opportunities. I thought I should make a kind of "Top 10" list, a GET OUT OF JAIL FREE card should the chance arise to, say, party and jam with George Clinton and the P-Funk All-Stars. I would flash my relapse pass to the heavens and say, "It's cool. I'm allowed to drink in this situation." But then I realized I hadn't listened to Parliament Funkadelic since college, and I don't actually play an instrument, so jamming would just be embarrassing. Really, Clinton and crew just seem like a fun bunch, but they're not actually relapse-worthy.

Alas, with my living celebrity relapse dance card empty, I thought I might plan for a more realistic scenario or two: like being forced at gunpoint to drink—or else. I've often had this dream where terrorists make me guzzle whiskey. In the dream, I fight the armed relapse agents, determined to preserve the months-long sobriety that I have worked so hard to achieve. But, in the end, I am tied to a chair and forced to chug Johnnie Walker while the gunmen practice their evil laughs. "You bashtards," I slur through tears as I realize I will have to start getting sober all over again.

    I would wake up from the dream with a start, so relieved that I still had my sobriety, that it was all in my head. But it has also occurred to me that, while I would of course truly be devastated by a forcible relapse, a very real part of me was practicing my own evil laugh. Somewhere in the sickest recesses of my alcoholism, a nasty little corner in my brain is still conniving, still scheming about how to get some hooch. Maybe if terrorists kidnap me . . .

Chapter 2

Other People's Drinking

The first time I hung out with Jack and Tessa since getting sober—it was November, and I had four months clean—I had a flashback to being the new kid in school. When my family moved from Albany to Syracuse (which is a little like staying in place), I was in third grade. The teacher, Mrs. Glenn, took me gently by the shoulders, steered me to the front of the class, smiled, and said, "Class, this is Sacha." "Hi, Sacha," came the bored chorus in classic grammar school call-and-response. It all seemed so familiar at first—the flip-top desks, the construction-paper murals, the chalk-dust air, the weird kid who eats paste and communicates solely through farm-animal noises. But then I felt the appraising eyes of the group, assessing what niche to sort me into, wondering what's up with that rainbow shirt (all the rage at my last school), and speculating as to whether there was anything good in my lunch box—or was I one of those loser kids for whom an apple counted as dessert? Jack and Tessa were both completely the same and totally unrecognizable. Not only was I the New Kid, I was the foreign-exchange student, dropping into an exotic subculture, practicing my language skills, and all the while dreaming of a home where I made more sense to the people around me. Tessa darted about nervously, and I, like the New Kid, hovered at the edges of the room trying to slip into the culture of the moment without drawing too much attention to myself or to the lame contents of my lunch box.

"So you don't want a beer, right?" asked Tessa. She meant it innocently; the idea of me no longer drinking was probably as strange and unbelievable as cats talking. Perhaps she thought I was just drastically cutting back. The word *sobriety* had not yet crossed my lips in front of my two best friends. And, in that moment, as moisture streaked down the side of the beer bottle, I thought, *Why not?* If I do this, then immediately, everything will go back to normal. I won't be the New Kid. The mist will lift, and we will instantly all know one another again. I watched Tessa carefully and noticed the devil clock I had given her as a gift for Christmas over her shoulder, its pointy goatee and shifty eyes ticking back and forth, marking the seconds. Tessa's hair had been dyed from fire-engine red to more of a deep purple recently. Purple Tess with the devil on her shoulder. The question had been hanging in the air too long: *So you don't want a beer, right?* I don't know if Jack saw the flurry of indecision that crossed my face or not, but he jumped in. "No, she can't have a beer; she's an alcoholic," he said, without any sense of irony. What's more, when Tessa then asked if I minded if she drank (her sweet voice betrayed by the panic behind her eyes), Jack interceded again. "She has to get used to people drinking around her," he exclaimed, grabbing a beer.

And so, Jack had saved me from a near relapse and simultaneously let me know that such support was limited, qualified by his own right to drink. In one sense, he was right, of course. I would have to learn to get used to people drinking around me. But just then, as I squinted against the spotlight of sobriety, I wanted nothing more than for my best friends to embrace me, to not use in front of me, to tell me they wanted to help. But this was crazy. After all, how many times had I myself sneered at the idea of teetotaling? When an ex-boyfriend once suggested that we cut back and get healthy, I smiled but thought, *Well, fuck. That's it for this relationship.* Whenever I met someone who didn't drink—or didn't drink much—I mentally erased her from my Potential Friends Database without bothering to learn anything else about her. I joked about sober alcoholics as "quitters" and "failures at drinking." And how many times had Jack, Tessa, and I all rolled our eyes together at the pearl-necklace-wearing squares who peopled so much of our fair city while we hoisted another?

Once, when Tessa and I were having linguine at Pasta Mia, I watched the other diners with calculation. *They're going home after dinner,* I thought. *This dinner is the main event for the night.* But, for me, Pasta Mia was just the prelude to a much longer and more colorful evening—maybe dancing, maybe five hours of *Twin Peaks.* And I felt sorry for these people, these twenty- and thirtysomethings who had so completely abandoned themselves to normalcy, doing neat impressions of adults as they nursed a single glass of wine and talked about real estate. Meanwhile, Tessa and I practically fell into our pasta bowls, screaming with laughter, tears streaming down our faces as we mapped out the great screenplay we should write: some kind of comedy-horror movie wherein a career gal at some point tosses her knit beret into the air à la Mary Tyler Moore only to get hit by a bus. I had visions of Jack, Tessa, and I sitting around, each with a laptop, co-writing our way to fame. It never occurred to me that the people at those other tables were already doing amazing things with their lives—they could be reporters, spies, human rights advocates (we were in D.C., after all). I preferred to think of them all as painfully dry working drones and myself as something more, well, special. Comeuppance is a bitch.

And versions of my former sneering self were everywhere. Like when the slinky intern at work who drank straight vermouth and smoked skinny cigarettes gasped, "You don't drink? *Ever?*" as though I had just told her I'd given up breathing air. What to say to that? Maybe: "Do you mean 'ever in my life' or 'ever after'—like from here on out?" But

instead I just stammered out, "Nope," and willed myself not
to add "But I'm still fun!" or cry.

After I told my hairdresser that I was an alcoholic, he
looked at me wryly as he back-combed my hair into something he would later, once satisfied, deem "kittenish," and
said, mock conspiratorially, "Oh God, me, too. I am *such* an
alcoholic." He may well be. But what he really meant is that
he currently drinks an awful lot and he would enjoy hanging
out with me, a kindred spirit, sometime—preferably while
wearing boas and watching *Grey Gardens*. This sort of thing
happens with surprising frequency, and ultimately I have to
tell this good-time Charlie that I am not being cheeky, that
I am an alcoholic in the Betty Ford sense of the word, not in
the bon vivant sense. And that is when, as though on cue,
I am usually treated to a quick and scattered story about
my hairdresser's alcoholic uncle/college roommate/cousin/
stepfather while simultaneously cementing my own place on
his mental "Never Hang Out with This Broad Again" list.

People just aren't prepared for the word "alcoholic" to actually apply to someone in their midst. Once, at an office
orientation, a group of new colleagues and I were asked to go
around the room and say a little something about ourselves.
After the usual banalities ("Hi, I'm Sarah; I work in human
resources," "Hi, I'm Mitch, and I work in development"),
the circle shifted to the googly-eyed dude with the puce
short-sleeved button-down shirt; he was practically beaming with excitement: "Hi, I'm Jeremy, and I'm an alcoholic!"

he squealed as the room shook with laughter, the fluorescent lights catching the tiny sweat globules on his pate. "No, seriously, I work in accounting . . ."

Now this is one of those moments where, if I really had any stones, I would laugh the loudest and the longest—still laughing after the rest of the bunch had settled down and started to look at me uncomfortably. "Hi-fucking-larious, Jeremy," I would say. "So you're not here for the twelve step meeting, then? Because I was really looking forward to your experience, strength, and hope." And then I would start laughing a little more, maybe clutch the hand of the person next to me as I exhaled. Then I'd turn back to Jeremy from accounting, sudden and serious: "It's awesome that you feel so at ease mocking alcoholics in the workplace, Jeremy. I especially like how Sarah from human resources seems to think this is a great joke, too. You are obviously a sophisticated and shrewd bunch." Then, while all eyes were still on me, I'd look directly and meaningfully at Jeremy: "Allow me to introduce myself. My name is Sacha, I work on the magazine, and I collect very, very sharp knives." But instead I just scowled, said my name, and privately swore to make any expense reports I had as complicated and half-assed as I possibly could for Jeremy in accounting.

So now I was on the other side of a joke from Jack and Tessa. I had tacitly agreed to one set of rules—where cocktails were always glued to our hands, where our lives did not rush forward but grooved along in an endless night, where

the tone was wicked and acerbic—and now I was changing
games completely. In the sunlight and dry, I felt utterly hu-
morless. As scatological yuks and cruel barbs flew through
Tessa's house that afternoon, I could no longer relate. I
thought of an old joke: You're funnier when I drink.

For many alcoholics, hanging out with old friends is impossible. Like going into a favorite watering hole where the
bartender makes your drink before you order it—where every
bottle on the bar back says, *Pick me!,* and promises an easier
night, a small escape from the cruel bathos of the day; where
you find yourself relaxing into it and thinking, *Ah, that's the
stuff*—so, too, hanging out with pals cues your brain into that
dark magic, a strange tapping on your frontal cortex (*Drink.
Drink. Drink.*), your friends as tempting as any siren's call.
And so drinking buddies are eschewed. Drinking buddies.
But Jack and Tessa were my closest friends, not some sketchy
dudes I ran into at the bars now and then.

Watching Jack and Tessa pull down gulps of cold beer
on a warm day while I chain-smoked and pounded Diet
Cokes with the unquenchable thirst of someone who has just
dragged herself out of the Sahara, I could not help but feel a
tad twitchy.

"I like what you've done with the place," said Jack as he
stared at the hole in Tessa's kitchen ceiling—or the hole in the
upstairs bathroom floor, depending on your point of view.

"Would you just hold him right there while I run upstairs
and pee on his head?" Tessa asked me.

"No! She'll give me the clap," squealed Jack. "Do you know why they call it the clap? Because 'Woo! I've got the clap!'" Jack said as he jumped up and down clapping like a teenage girl who just made the cheer squad.

"I knew you had the clap, you skanky slut," said Tessa, backing away.

"Why you gotta be so nasty?" said Jack, reaching for her. "I don't actually have the clap," he said meaningfully to me as he lunged for Tessa, clasping her in a bear hug and running his "clap-infested" hands across her face while she screamed, "Stop, whore!" Jack held her squirming body firmly and whispered, "Shh, you love it."

I wondered: Is it possible to feel nostalgia while you are in the midst of the very situation you are nostalgic for? It was not yet easy to be uninhibited and playful—and sober. It was bawdy, it was lewd, but we loved each other. I felt like a person who had been on a decades-long journey returning home to things and people both familiar and fond but with too much distance coursing between us. In the months before I quit drinking, I had burrowed into booze, phoning Jack and Tessa only when it suited me, only when drunk or to ask them to get drunk, and only to focus on the state of *my* soul—never theirs (when they called me, I ignored the phone or gave pithy responses about being "busy"). At times, I could be a torrent of neediness and solipsism, sucking Jack and Tessa dry and discarding the bones. And yet, that day in November, it did not yet occur to me that Jack and Tessa might be treating me carefully because *I* had hurt *them*. I simply and conveniently blamed my sobriety for any chill in the air.

Throughout the afternoon, we caught up with each other's lives. I heard about Jack's new boyfriend and Tessa's plan to move to Baltimore, about the adventures of mutual friends, and highlights from the last few months. But I felt like I could not tell them anything about the most significant event in my life. I may have wanted them to stroke my forehead and tell me I was still their girl, but I never gave them the chance. I never allowed them to adapt to the new me, because I never breathed a word about what was really going on with me.

"You okay?" asked Tessa.

Was I? Well, let's see: I had started eating bowls of ice cream as big as my head every night after dinner, I couldn't fathom where one would hang out on a beautiful summer day if not the patio of a bar, I was sitting here smoking cigarettes even though I had quit because, hell, I mean I had to do *something*, I had white-knuckled my way through a dinner party where I started to get weepy every time someone offered me a glass of wine, and I was so tweaked out on caffeine lately that my eyeballs throbbed. But, worst of all, I decided that I couldn't share any of this with my friends. Because no matter what—as much I wanted to let Jack and Tessa in, to give them the honest truth, to be vulnerable—the last thing in the world I could allow myself to be was a buzzkill. I may have ruined my good time, but damn it, I would not ruin theirs!

And it did not enter my mind that they might care a lot less about that than I did. So I lied.

"I'm great," I replied to Tessa in a fake voice and a small forced smile.

What I didn't say was that booze is fucking everywhere. I can't walk home without running into it. In the one-mile walk from *Reader's Digest* to my apartment, I counted more than twenty bars. I turn on the television, and every show I watch is set in a bar and every ad is for a new liquor. I want to tell them this, but do not. I want to tell them I see booze like the kid in the movie sees dead people—a haunting spectacle on every corner. And no one is drinking it! Chardonnay glasses are idling for forty-five minutes at a time on café tables across the city as we speak. And of course those few who are drinking look lushy and fragmented and a lot like how I imagine I looked a few months back: Not only am I seeing alcohol everywhere; I am seeing alcoholics everywhere.

In fact, just ten days into sobriety, I had gone to a journalism awards dinner at the National Press Club with a group of colleagues from *Reader's Digest*. Wineglasses littered the table, seemingly dozens per place setting, with an army of caterers breathing down my neck. The waiters, who all seemed to look like John Waters—with pencil-thin moustaches and extravagant sidelong glances—skated by tables and snarled, "Red or white?" So I began to turn the massive cluster of wineglasses near my plate upside-down—all, I don't know, forty or fifty of them. Was that a water glass? Who cares?! Was that my neighbor's glass? Too suspicious—it must be over-turned! Once I had created a kind of stemware archipelago—stem-side up—I noticed I was attracting glances from my *Digest* colleagues. So I hunkered down behind my crystal for-tress, watched my colleagues' faces turn Picasso-esque through the glassware, and ate all the goat cheese off my salad.

As the evening's main event got underway and the emcee handed out statuettes, I began to realize that I, too, would like an award. I had not been personally nominated for an award, of course; other, less interesting people at the *Digest* were the ones nominated. (Happy to accept an award I didn't earn? Classic alcoholic.) Still, I kept irrationally hoping that my name would be called, perhaps for a searing puppy-mill exposé or parakeet-trafficking report—all of the winners seemed to be animal stories. Maybe this would be the year that I became a crackerjack kitty-cat columnist, heralded both for saving the poor feral felines and doing it with such flair. "You okay, babe?" asked my boss, Kate. The "babe" was a trick, an informality that did little to hide the barracuda doing laps beneath the surface of her skin. (This is a woman who once told me that media was like a blood sport and I should ignore the wussy men we worked with and just follow her lead.) "Super," I said with a sudden and toothy smile; I felt it was important to be "super" around work people.

Meanwhile, my mind was racing. When I wasn't plotting how to win acclaim from my peers as an animal journalist, I was counting drinks: Kate, one glass white plus a refill she hadn't yet touched; Jonah, two reds; Dina, one red; Mike, one scotch from the bar, one white, untouched. And, when the count remained roughly the same a half an hour later, I received further confirmation of my own lusty alcoholism. These people were *nursing* their drinks, refusing refills, and generally not paying any attention at all to the booze right in front of them. *Mommy still loves you*, I thought as I longingly eyed all the neglected glasses and half-portions going to waste before my eyes. *For heaven's sake, people, there are starving children in Africa. Drink your wine!*

Later, as we all left the table, I noticed that, to a person, every seat at the table—save mine—had a half-empty glass in front of it. My plate, on the other hand, ensconced in crystal goblets, looked like Superman's lair. I hung back and watched my colleagues filter out into the room; not one of them finished their drink before departing. This was new to me: Ten days earlier, I would have happily left half my entrée, all of my mushrooms, and part of my dessert behind, but goddamn it, I would have downed that last glass of wine before I left—and it wouldn't have been my second of the night. I felt like they had left something important behind, like each had left a purse or wallet on their chairs. "You forgot to drink your wine!" I wanted to shout after them. Christ, at least drink one for me.

Before Sobriety, I had rarely considered how much or how little the people around me were drinking. Now, stripped of my nectar, I couldn't help but obsess over exactly how much everyone around me was putting back. When Peter noticed our friend Aden swaying and slurring one evening after a dinner party and said, "I didn't think Aden had that much to drink," I could remind him of the two Maker's Marks that Aden downed *before* we even started dinner, the two he had with dinner, and the two glasses of some new bottle of wine the host made everyone except me try. Also, at 11:05 Cara ordered a glass of champagne, which wasn't relevant to Aden's consumption but which I found an interesting choice and decided to point out. It was like a superpower—one I sense Peter is jealous of, as he always rolls his eyes at such moments and says silly things like, "You sure?" Sure?! It's burned into my brain; it's a superpower, after all—an alcohol-cataloguing superpower that is never wrong. So, you know, shut up.

In fact, after one evening out with my future brother-in-law, I knew that he, too, was an alcoholic—before everyone else did. I was uncomfortably white-knuckling my way through a family dinner out at a restaurant at a couple months sober when I watched Stephen have three cocktails before the salads were done, more glasses of wine than anyone else once the entrée arrived, and a spiked coffee with dessert (which he tried to hide, ordering coffee along with everyone else and then sort of coughing out, "Make it Irish," to the waiter); Steve followed this up with port back at his folks' apartment and, when that was gone, rummaged around in the fridge for a beer (back left, behind the green pitcher; I'd done a hard-target search in this icebox once myself). As I was in early sobriety, my superpowers were at their peak, and I knew something the rest did not: People in this family do not drink that much—and not in this situation. I was aware of how Stephen would nod to his empty glass when the waiter slid by rather than ask for more out loud. I watched as he ordered another glass of wine à la carte when the bottle was gone. And of course I noticed the clumsily ordered spiked coffee. He had tried to hide it, but the semicoherent *cough, cough, Make it Irish*, wasn't in the snooty waiter's ken. "Excuse me, sir?" the waiter said, extending a moment Stephen had hoped to cruise right through, ensuring that all eyes were now on Stephen as he ordered his coffee. "Put some Baileys in the coffee," Stephen said through the corner of his mouth. I felt his thoughts then: that maybe his parents didn't know what Irish coffee was or what Baileys was, and that they had yet to notice how much he had consumed already. I scoffed inside; he was being so obvious. But he was right: His folks didn't bat an eye. When the coffee came, Steve made a big show of satisfaction after the first sip. "Ah, that's good. It's good to have coffee, wake us up a little." As though he were drinking regular coffee with the rest of us; as though his coffee were simply caffeinated and not spiked; as though, if he drew attention to the coffee part of the drink, we would all forget the Baileys part. A classic diversion—one I saw now worked better for the drinker than the intended audience, like when I drank mimosas and then mentioned how it felt good to have a healthy glass of juice. I was like a child who had to have carrot shavings tossed into her macaroni-and-cheese in order to get a modicum of vegetables into her diet. *See this Cape Cod? Sure, there's vodka in it, but there's also a full serving of vitamin C in every glass!* Back home, as he drank port and beer, I tried to ignore the mirror Steve was holding up to me. I put my head down and powered through the evening while a nasty brew of rage, jealousy, disgust, and envy coursed through my veins. I smiled at my future mother-in-law. *I'm a good girl, I swear.* I prayed she would never see me the way I saw myself just then.

Often average, non-problem-drinking people will think someone is just having a big night or that they are, in general, a big drinker—no doubt there are those—but non-problem-drinking people aren't immune to knowing, even loving, addicts. There are millions of us, after all. Of course, the non-problem-drinkers are always the last to know—mainly because they aren't collecting, cataloguing, and mentally filing away an entire evening's repertoire of drinks. But I am! You're welcome.

The good news is that Stephen has been sober for several years now (no thanks to my acute powers of observation) and is often a comrade-in-arms at family functions, his presence a comforting reminder of our mutual battle. The bad news is that I lost my superpower. In time, my daily obsession with alcohol would fade into a dark bog in my mind, morphing into more of an obsession with plotting my relapse. Nevertheless, lesson learned: Non-addicts don't care much at all about alcohol, can turn down drinks at will, can leave half-empty glasses behind, and think nothing of going a few nights without. Meanwhile, I had the number of the Chinese takeout place that delivered beer, chardonnay, and cigarettes after 2 A.M. committed to memory. (I'd always order a small fried rice as well, so the delivery guy didn't think I was a total alcoholic or anything.)

"You sure you're great?" Tessa asked.

Not even close. But what could I say? I was sitting on a nuclear-armed missile and all I had to do was whisper the secret launch code—*I've noticed that most people don't really drink that much*—and I'd blow us all to hell.

"Totally sure," I said.

At least, I assumed I would blow us all to hell. It did not strike me that my friends were not as interested in drinking as I was; nor did it strike me that telling them about how little most people drank would not ruin their day at all. Because I saw all of our interactions through the prism of alcohol, I assumed they did as well. I had systematically pigeonholed them into a category of Wild and Crazy Friend and did not give them a chance to be anything else.

That was the first time we all hung out—just the three of us—since I stopped drinking. So far, it has also been the last. Sobriety has brought me closer to every single other person in my life—except Jack and Tessa. And it is entirely my fault. For years, I had toyed with the idea of dropping out of my career, getting a job at a bar, and devoting my life to enjoying my friends. But now that a life of partying had revealed itself to be less than idyllic, now that the panic attacks I had endured for years had simply and miraculously disappeared in sobriety, now that my vision for my future was a bigger dream than I had ever allowed myself, I changed games. I crossed enemy lines. I betrayed my drunken nation. Or so I thought. I never entertained the possibility that they did not feel betrayed.

Still, I no longer know how to tell Jack and Tessa everything, to bare my soul. How do I tell them that I feel awake while they are mixing drinks? I wonder if they miss me: Is the party the same without me? I wonder if they judge me. I know that they get together without me, that I am no longer essential to the team, that I might in fact spoil the good time. Or maybe, they get together without me, not because they still party like we all used to. Maybe they get together without me because I have become a skittish kitten around them, ignoring phone calls and excusing myself as interminably too busy to hang out. Because, unfortunately, when I do see Jack and Tessa, I see my former self—the chick who had wild highs and sobbing streaks; the chick who dove into k-holes, threw back booze recklessly, and didn't see the difference between weeknights and weekends; the chick who rolled her eyes at sincerity and was suspicious of nondrinkers—and I don't know how to introduce them to the new me, to the new kid in school. I have—without their permission—made them the psychic symbols of my "Before" picture. I have even been scared of them, of their boundless freedom. Still, I love them.

In my twenties, when I would visit my parents for a week, I'd return to my D.C. apartment to find it covered in WELCOME BACK signs hand-drawn by Tessa. When I didn't answer my phone for hours on end, Jack would be knocking down my door to make sure I was all right. When I had to meet up with an acquaintance I hadn't seen in years and was nervous about it, Jack and Tessa would tag along and make an evening of it. I never had to be alone. I never had to face any situation, however mundane, without the legion of support they had at the ready just for me. But now I am new. And, even when I miss them desperately, I am frightened they will not like this new me—a woman who tosses around earnest concepts like "authenticity" with surprising effortlessness. I am so frightened they will not like this new me, I have never given them the chance to decide for themselves. And I have never given myself the chance to find out if they also have grown or changed. And surely they have.

Sometimes, I feel like I am watching Jack and Tessa from the rear window of a car that's pulling away. They are having fun without me, while I am driven to something completely unknown.

Number 2 on the Sacha Fantasy Relapse Pass: Time Machine

The scientist at the time-machine laboratory thanks me for agreeing to participate in his study. He has the shock of gray and white hair you'd expect from your classic evil-genius time-machine creator, but he also has the unnerving habit of twitching when he speaks.

"You'd be surprised [twitch] at how few people [twitch] want to travel back in time [twitch]," the scientist stammers. I sense, however, that people are more afraid of allowing this dude to put them in a small, blinking box than they are afraid of time travel itself. But not me. Even as I eye the box warily, smoke is wafting out from under the hatch door ("It's perfectly [twitch] safe [twitch]"), but I can think of nothing better than traveling backward. To just gently back away, back before sobriety.

The scientist impresses upon me that I can only travel back in my own past; I can only revisit my own memories. That means the sixties are out—no Woodstock; no beatnik poetry café; no turning on, tuning in, and dropping out—which is disappointing. It also means none of the seventies or eighties discos, cocaine, egoism, and glitter, as I was too young for such pursuits at the time, which is also disappointing. The nineties are an option, I suppose, but honestly I don't think I should waste my time-travel ride on Lollapalooza, 'shrooms, camping, and grunge.

I missed out on the dot-com bubble and was often the only partier surrounded by upwardly mobile friends in the nineties. No, I crave something a bit bigger than the slacker microbrews and Nirvana videos of my fellow Generation Xers. But then, the new millennium wasn't all bad to me, was it? I smile at the scientist: "I'm ready."

The scientist puts me into the box and sticks several small electrodes to my head. It smells like sulfur in the box, which is completely white save for the odd blinking button ("Do not [twitch] touch [twitch] the buttons [twitch]"). The scientist asks me to concentrate on a memory:

. . . Tessa's living room is lit in dull orange tones that catch the shimmer in our cheeks. We are flush, excited, and gorgeous. Tessa, Jack, and I sit in a small circle looking at our stash: There are bottles of wine and vodka, a gallon of cranberry juice, several limes, a mirror with a pile of cocaine, some Ecstasy, and a small wad of marijuana. We smile knowingly at one another in anticipation . . .

I want one more ride on the roller coaster. One more evening with the funniest people I know. One more night to lose my legs on the dance floor and my mind on the crest of a drug-fueled wave. I want to see Jack's and Tessa's faces flash by me in the dark, I want to hear their laughter, I want to feel the unspeakable joy of the surrender. I want to drink with them, play with them, just one last time—more than I've ever wanted to drink with anybody else.

"I've got it," I tell the scientist quietly, trying not to lose the thread, the feeling of that memory.

The scientist lowers the hatch on the time machine.

"Just don't forget to pull me out before the paroxysm of terror and paranoia," I shout at the scientist. "That'll be around 5 A.M., just as I start to break out in hives."

Chapter 3
The Ghost in the Chair

I knew I loved Peter when he left a book at my doorstep. Halloween was nearing, the neighborhood smelled like wet leaves, and in the moonlight I saw a note on my front door: READ IF YOU DARE. I didn't know Peter very well yet, but when I saw *House of Leaves* waiting for me—a cult horror novel that you can only read to the point that you are either scared out of your gourd and shivering in the corner or else driven utterly mad and left cursing the dozens of pages of labyrinthine footnotes, whichever comes first—I had only one thought: *Fuck, yeah.*

By day, Peter has the cool detachment of a great leader; his commanding baritone enters the conversation before his words, impressing upon you, "Listen up, I, Peter, am now speaking." He wears cuff links and a tie when others are in jeans and sweaters. His unflinching devotion to logic and reason give him clearheaded purpose in a town of spin. And, though he was born and raised in Manhattan, when I imagine him speaking, I hear him in a British accent. "Rubbish!" he yells at the op-ed page of the newspaper. "My God, man, have you gone completely mad?!" Peter is not actually a Brit, but somewhere in his soul lurks an intellectual Englishman with a fondness for foreign affairs, empiricism, realism, and Thomas Pink shirts.

By night, however, Peter will eschew back issues of *Arms Control Today* to consume a frightening number of B movies and books—science fiction, horror, or thriller—preferably endeavors with titles like *Mansquito*. He will also don motorcycle boots, blast Metallica, and headbang in a full hesher symphony of attitude and rage. In addition to Barack Obama, William F. Buckley, and George Kennan, Metallica lead vocalist James Hetfield (or simply James, as he is known in our house) would be high on Peter's list of people he would like to have dinner with, living or dead.

And the more I came to know and continue to know Peter, the more I see the secret layers, the special kinds of crazy that are only discovered when true intimacy is attained. Like how Peter forms sentimental attachments to most objects.

"What's that?" I ask, pointing at the boxy machine in the closet. "A toaster?"

"That's the laptop I wrote my junior thesis on," he replies, wistfully.

"I didn't have a laptop in college," I said. "Just a huge

box that was more of a fancy typewriter—and a vehicle for Q*Bert."

"Not in college," Peter said. "That was for my high school junior thesis."

"You wrote a junior thesis in high school?"

Of course, he did. Peter went to an amazing boarding school outside Boston—where he studied Chinese and, apparently, wrote a junior thesis on the negotiations at Yalta. Meanwhile, over in my hometown of Syracuse, New York, my classmates and I were getting high under the bleachers from bongs crafted in 3-D art class, all too aware that, with college acceptances already under our belts, none of this high school shit mattered anymore and we could traipse through these last months not only without learning a thing, but with the opportunity to actually hinder our lifetime potentials and pare back our brain cells. Good times.

"So we can recycle it?" I ask, tentatively poking the manila brick before us; this thing is probably made of radon.

"Nooo!" exclaims Peter as he lunges protectively toward the vault that once carried his prescient teenage thoughts on the development of the postwar world order.

"Okay, well what about this Pets-dot-com dog hand puppet?"

"Nooo!"

Still, peeling the onion of Peter's brain is far less terrifying than exposing my own layers of insanity and neurosis. As it was, for months in the first year of sobriety, the epiphanies issued forth, contorting my face into wide-eyed "Aha!" expressions that compelled Peter to say, "What is it?!" with a kind of hurried excitement. I then had to admit whatever invariably mundane blast of realization had just popped up, such as "It just occurred to me that I used to drink a lot, like *a lot.*" Duh. I dared not admit to Peter the really ugly stuff, like how I used to lie as easily as I breathed ("I'm so happy for you!") and had a one-hour-on/one-hour-off work ethic. And I started to feel that I needed a hand navigating nonalcoholic waters.

In the pursuit of self-knowledge, I started going to a twelve-step meeting. I expected to find a room full of ex-hipsters with sleeve tattoos and piercings. I thought that, when the party ended, I'd find scene-makers, club-goers, and concert-followers; I expected it to look a little like last call at watering holes like the Black Cat, the 9:30 Club, or Wonderland—the mini-Brooklyns of Washington, D.C. But, when I stepped into the room, which was aboveground and not at a church, I was met with a group of ordinary people, a simple cross section of the city. Like jury duty. And I wondered, *Where are all the punk rockers?*

As the meeting came to life around me, I felt obvious in my newness and unconnected to the people in folding chairs scattered throughout the room. I just showed up and people took turns talking about their feelings. Was I expected to do the same? Shouldn't there be some kind of orientation meeting? I wanted a *Twelve-Step for Dummies.* I felt like an idiot. It took everything I had to approach someone after the meeting, but I did. I needed the lowdown. I needed someone to verify that I should be there, because I was not very sure at all. I chose the woman who had laughed the loudest: Amy, a beautiful woman with a salt-and-pepper buzz-cut, perfect makeup, and five-inch high heels who oozed a kind of ruthless cool. Amy shook her head, smiling, while I explained that I used to drink a lot and was deciding whether or not I could do it alone. "Oooooh, Lordy," she said, while I shrank into my seat. "God sent you to me for a reason." That was one "God" and one "Lordy." I wasn't sure I liked her after all. I told her I wasn't going to pray. She laughed and told me to keep going to meetings and not to worry about praying—yet.

So, I sat in twelve-step meetings and coffee shops— addicts' favorite haunts—like a ghost, just a shell of a formerly lively personality who now was starting to see just how exceptionally unoriginal she was. I used to think of myself as a very exciting person whom people wanted to be around. But now I saw that they only wanted to be around me up to a point; I was fun for an evening but not much longer. After a while, I'd only meet you if it was for drinks or just avoid you altogether, I wouldn't keep in touch very well if at all, and I never really remembered what was going on in your world. I began to think about all the alcoholics who came before me in life who had also quit drinking. I began to feel wholly banal. I looked back at my B.S. time and I didn't see a charming party girl who delighted everyone who met her ("Sacha's here! She's crazy!"); I saw a cliché: DRUNK CHICK GETS THRILLS FROM SHOCKING THE NORMS AND FEELING SUPERIOR; PUKES AT 11. How many people in this coffee shop were also alcoholics? Perhaps in the very chair I was sitting in right then sat another alcoholic an hour earlier having similar epiphanies. Perhaps an hour before that yet another alcoholic did the same. Here we all were wandering the city like specters, not fully our whole selves yet, as we sipped coffee and thought about who we were without the alcohol. And who we weren't: fun people.

Often when I met other people in sobriety, I found myself recognizing their stories, their struggles, their hilariously flawed thinking—like how it's not drinking alone if you have a pet. And for a long time that actually made me feel worse. I wasn't unique anymore. I wasn't in Neverland anymore, laughing at the rest of the world with Jack and Tessa. I was out in that place called "the rest of the world" and seeing my past more clearly. It wasn't so sparkly and cool to me anymore; it was bloated and wan, irresponsible and entitled, catty and snarky, all talk and no action. Not only wasn't I unique, I wasn't sure I was even a good person. I wasn't sure I'd been a good person for a long time.

In college at Columbia University, I started asking, "What if?"—as though I were some kind of scientist, as though I boasted some genuine curiosity about the world. What if I squeeze saltwater and dish soap into the coin slot of the dorm's vending machine? Answer: dozens of stolen sodas in every flavor, one broken soda machine, and one newly installed security camera. Fascinating! Make a note! What if I join the campus communists and read (okay, purchase) books by Trotsky? Answer: Unfortunately, this experiment was abandoned after lunchtime cocktails and ended in an emergency capitalist spree at the Urban Outfitters in the Village. What if I go drink-for-drink with the six-foot-four, 250-pound senior sitting next to me? Answer: I puke—which sobers me enough that I can drink even more. Excellent! What if I just skip all my finals this semester? Answer: I flunk out of school, piss off my parents, and am forced to finish my education somewhere less, heh, expensive. And that, really, I think it is safe to say, is the moment when the *what ifs* stopped and the *fuck its* began. I stopped asking questions and started answering them.

I had given up my Ivy League education in a fog of depression and alcohol. The more I drank, the more I wanted to sleep. The more I slept, the more classes I missed. The more classes I missed, the guiltier I felt. And the guiltier I felt, the more I drank. I spun wildly in this black and demented round-robin until every college rite I had pursued—from my philosophy classes to the parliamentary debate team— began to recede from view. I wanted to be an honors student, I wanted debating trophies, I wanted a successful life predicated on a successful college career. But what I wanted, I also sabotaged at every turn. And, instead of recognizing that all of my actions had predictable consequences, I just went ahead and assumed that I was not smart enough to handle an Ivy League school. I was a public school city kid from 'Cuse; what had I been thinking anyway?

"I'm going to start collecting Molson Black Ice beer bottle caps and Molson Golden caps and make a chessboard," says the baseball-hat-wearing non-jock slacker next to me at a Binghamton University college bar as he sizes up the contrasting cap hues before him. I yawn. He continues, "It's gonna be awesome. Wanna get scorpion bowls and see who can finish first?" I look at him with interest for the first time that night as I do the math: I do not like him, his friends, or even my own new friends my senior year at my new college— nor, for that matter, do I like my new college, banished as I am back in upstate New York. I should not prolong this night. "Fuck it," I say and grab a straw, knowing that right now all that matters is horking down this bowl of red Drano before this nine-year-old tries to explain to me from which part of the beer bottle the men for his chessboard will be made. And so it goes: It's a school night. Fuck it. I'm dropping out of law school. Fuck it. I have a deadline. Fuck it. It's a work night. Fuck it. I'm at work right now. Fuck it.

I mistook my free fall for freedom. I thought the absence of boundaries defined me. How far could I go? How low? And now I saw the pain of a soured life, the exhaustion of a life too rushed and ill-considered. For years, I felt sure I bore some deep psychosis. I had a double soul that pulled me maniacally between the rush of saying, "Fuck It, Fuck It, Fuck It," and the pulsing desire to pursue a career, to be a success, to travel, to take pride in myself. I alternately nurtured fantasies of waitressing in some sleepy beach town or else launching my own magazine. I trudged on in the real world, detesting mornings, slogging through stress, pummeling away at the necessary steps to a Career. And I drank and drank and drank. I did everything the hard way and, instead of acknowledging that I couldn't live in two worlds, I told myself that I had a double soul, that I had an internal doppelganger, that I wasn't built like other people, that I was flawed, unlike other people. A unique diagnosis: I was special. (Maybe I needed a *special*ist!) If Peter or anyone else were to peel back the layers of Sacha, they would find two people: the one they loved and the vampire, who lived for nights and who sucked all the life out of you in lieu of taking care of herself.

Once on the subway in New York City, I saw another double soul: a young man turned slightly away from me. It was late, and the fluorescent lights saturated the car in a jaundiced glow. There were a thousand reasons why I should not have been on the subway alone at night, but the only one I could think of at that moment was how awful I must look in this light. The young man across from me was handsome and long, with legs that stretched into the middle of the car as he reclined. He wore a beautiful and obviously expensive brown suede coat and a pair of charcoal jeans. He looked so put together. I hate it when men are too stylish; it's impossible to date someone who dresses better than you. Next to him, I felt like a costumed little girl in my Doc Martens and J.Crew sweater. I tried to look cool in my twenties, but somehow a J.Crew sweater always showed up, clinging to me of its own volition while my tough-girl boots sneered. Meanwhile, the tall drink of water on the subway looked just plain elegant. What's the opposite of emasculating?

Yet, it was as he shifted in his seat that the man really drew my attention; his suede coat fell open and his head swung around. And, though we had never met, I knew exactly who he was. His open coat revealed a tight red sequined halter top, the delicate ruffles of an apparently unstuffed black bra peeking out at the top. He wore a tiny choker necklace with little jingle bells around it. As he pulled his head up, his now exposed ear presented a huge rhinestone earring dangling like a disco ball from his weighted lobe. The bright lighting conspired to reveal tiny traces of makeup across his face—liner around his gray-blue eyes and shimmer along his cheekbones. His red-pink lips were like candy. He was heartbreakingly beautiful. *I know you*, I thought. I so badly wanted to take his hand and tell him I knew.

I imagined his parents. They lived in a well-to-do apartment on the Upper East Side, the kind of building with marbled halls and domed ceilings that send shivers of longing down any ordinary person's spine. His parents had seen their son on Christmas, perhaps wearing the same neutral charcoal jeans, and they had given him the suede coat as a gift. They were good to him and they wanted their son to be warm. When the holiday was over, the turkey eaten, the good wine toasted, and the presents exchanged, he donned the suede coat to the delight of his mother (*He likes it!*) and kissed his folks good-bye. They smiled to one another as their good son left the fold once more, never guessing that he had a secret life downtown, a life that made him a woman from time to time in the smoky din of his favorite bar, a life that made him two people at once, the man he was and the woman he could be, a life that he could not resolve neatly nor express in the same way to all the same people. But I knew him. I knew his quiet nervousness as he approached his parents. I knew his fear of their reactions. I knew also his pain of living in a world of hushed words and secret dreams, where the tension between his two lives was as suffocating as it was intoxicating. And I suddenly felt very far away then, hidden underground with another underground comrade, and I relished my freedom. As long as we remained on the subway together, we were free from contradiction, safe on the train. I breathed out slowly.

He noticed me staring at him and he broke my reverie when in an embarrassed and altogether too deep voice he said, "Some of my buddies and I dressed up as girls for this party that we went to tonight." I didn't move; I was stunned. What do you do when your idols let you down? When they break your heart and leave you for dead? *You're on your own now, kid. You're all alone underground.* What happens when

59

a fellow traveler sneers at all you hold dear? I could barely contain my disappointment. Not only wasn't he who I had thought; he was embarrassed that I might have thought it. Where had my friend gone? My subway transsexual? Myself?

The man stood to get off at the next stop, walking to the doors in a kind of Neanderthal lope, a horrid macho walk that made him seem not elegant but spoiled, entitled, mocking. He wiped at his eyes as the doors parted and he left, probably to go listen to a little Kid Rock and slip a roofie into some unsuspecting woman's drink.

And there I was, steeped in my own lonely subterranean pain. Still, for a lost moment, I had been complete as I watched the man on the subway transform into something magic, something beautiful, something way better than reality, and for that moment I was euphoric. I was so euphoric I could taste the sweetness; I could even be the sweetness. I'm not a double soul. None of us are double souls. Not me, not even my subway transsexual (as I imagined him; not the ass-hat who thinks putting on makeup is kooky fun). I didn't need a specialist because I wasn't special. I was simply a whole person tearing herself in two and pretending that she was the victim of some rare disorder. How grandiose!

Living like two people had been my choice and living as one whole person would have to be as well. I had to choose sides. And choosing sobriety gave me myself back; without having to hide one set of friends from another set, without having to juggle work and partying, without having to tend to hangovers as part of my morning routine, without having to worry that my worlds would collide, I could be a single solitary person without the vampire inside. I knew who I wasn't supposed to be—barely employable, unproductive, financially reckless, unreliable, a liar. Now I could try and find out who I was supposed to be. I could peel the old onion. I could show Peter my subway-transsexual side—and maybe he'd even stick around.

It didn't occur to me that Peter would also have to change. I stopped drinking in June, and it was a hard fucking summer. Peter took over as acting editor of *The New Republic* while a colleague went on book leave, and he found himself in pitched battles with the magazine's owner that left him drained. One night, he looked through me, jaw clenched, as he poured himself a drink. No mercy. His body language was clear: *I'm not the alcoholic; I can have a drink.* I locked myself in the bathroom; I couldn't watch. I curled up on the floor in tears. I couldn't be someone new in an old situation. Not for the last time in sobriety, I clenched my fists and tried to muscle through. My heartbeat echoed in the little room, and I pressed my cheek to the cold tile. And here I had thought getting sober meant I'd never be splayed out on the bathroom floor again.

When I emerged from the bathroom, Peter was waiting just outside the door. "I'm sorry," he said as he scooped me up, his face in my hair, his breath on my cheek. "I'm so sorry."

With his arms gripping me almost tighter than I could bear, I could only think of all the trouble I'd caused: the needless fights I'd started as I threw back a couple bottles of wine, the nights I didn't call or even come home, and, worse, how many extra drinks had I encouraged him to drink in order to make me feel normal? "We'll figure it out," I said, knowing more than ever that he wasn't the one who should be sorry.

I once read that the only way to "cure" a sociopath is to show him that his behavior is no longer working for him. Forget convincing him that, say, murdering kittens is immoral or that it breaks little girls' hearts; forget making him feel empathy for his victims or teaching him the error of his ways. In time, a sociopath may begin to follow society's rules not because he learns to respect them, but because he knows violating those rules may just be more hassle than it's worth; breaking the rules might mean a headache he doesn't need. So the "cured" sociopath finally adapts to society because he realizes it is simply in his interest to do so, because, hell, it's easier—not because he's a new man. Acknowledging that I needed to get sober was a little like that. I just was so exhausted, so tired of the consequences of drinking, so over the hassle, the headache, the hangover, the insanity of it all, I said, *Okay, okay, I give up. I'll play by new rules.* But it didn't take long before—unlike a sociopath—my conscience rebooted, and I started to see how much of my life had been stained by alcohol. I started to wake up a little once I was living in the new rules of society, the new rules of sobriety, and

Unwasted

I saw that my addict behavior wasn't simply about drinking or not drinking. I, like all addicts, have a different personality architecture than non-addicts, one that's there whether I feed it with booze or not, one that seems bafflingly immature in the light of day.

"We'll figure it out," I repeated to Peter. "Also, there's mold on the bathroom ceiling."

Figuring it out became a months-long dance that ended with Peter drinking rarely and me meeting Amy regularly; she became my twelve-step sponsor, a guide to Planet Sober. (It is nice to have a cool soul sister who doesn't blink when I call her at midnight from out of town to talk about the cocktail party I just suffered through: "Sometimes I feel like the world is hoisting a martini, exhaling in delight, and saying, *This is what you can't have*." "What else is new?" says Amy.) That Peter seems to prefer me sober confounds the version of me who I thought was so much more fun when drinking, but makes perfect sense to Sacha 2.0, who can see just how much nicer and saner she is now. Sometimes, when we're watching a horror movie and fear and adrenaline are coursing through me, I look over at Peter and think that I've never felt safer. It's not that I need him to feel safe; it's that I can show him every part of me, even the dark bits, without scaring him off. Of course, it's easier to feel safe with someone else when you feel safe with yourself, when you've staked the vampire and taken to the daylight.

Watching Jack and Tessa, colleagues, and strangers

63

drink had been one thing. But that summer night—when I watched Peter pour a drink and then immediately fled to the bathroom—I felt like I was being kicked off Earth, left to float in space, untethered and adrift in the wildest, deepest black night. But then, maybe I needed to be unmoored for a while—to *feel* horrible instead of drink through the horrible. Maybe I needed to stop hanging on so tightly—to booze, to drugs, to anyone who would let me glom on. Maybe I needed to Let Go. That evening, as I wrestled with what it meant to not be able to throw some whiskey down the hatch after a bad day, I lay back on the bathroom floor and floated up into space like a lost astronaut, spiraling around in my space suit. But I wasn't alone. I took my subway transsexual with me. "We're as far from underground as we can get, buddy," I said. He smiled sweetly and held my hand in his own thick space-suit mitten while the stars rushed by and Earth receded. "Space is surprisingly painful," he whispered in a delicate voice. "But better, too."

Number 3 on the Sacha Fantasy Relapse Pass: A Shack of My Own

"You'll be sorry when I'm dead!" I scream at my boss, at Peter, at my friends, and at my family just before I am struck by a city bus.

I wake up in the hospital to find all of the people in my

*life weeping over my battered body. "Please forgive us,"
they cry. "We are so sorry!"*

*They should be sorry. It was all of their hectoring
and constant expectations—their insistence on things
like "paying my own rent," "getting up for work in the
morning," and "taking a shower"—that drove me from
them and out into the street where the city bus found
me. If it wasn't for all of these interfering friends, family, and colleagues and their ceaseless neediness, I'd be
fine. But, with them, it's always phone calls on birth-
days, retirement saving, deadlines, punctuality, health
food, and thank-you notes. You're either staying late at
work or getting there early; shopping for gift baskets for
the latest gaggle of baby showers, house-warmings, and
going-away parties or shopping for sanity with the latest
round of self-help, self-care, and self-preservation books,
balms, and baubles. There's no time to make lunch ahead
of time, no time to eat right, to walk the dog, to get to the
gym, to have energy, to appear happy, to make an appearance. But all of these people want something from
me, and it just got to be too much.*

*"Please forgive us," they cry over my hospital bed. "We
are so sorry!"*

*But I don't forgive them. I turn over in my hospital
bed and savor the pleasure of their pain. And of my own
relief: The project that was due, hanging over my head
like a guillotine—they'll have to handle it without me*

now. That party with college friends I wasn't thin enough for—they'll have to get by without me. The bills that were due, the appointments that were made, the checklist that was unchecked—all will float away for now. Because, for now, I must convalesce.

"Please forgive us," they cry once more, sensing my rejection. "We are so sorry!"

But I still don't forgive them. Instead, I move to a shack in the woods and drink. I take comfort in knowing they have driven me to this, with their nasty negative nagging and needling. There is no more office to return to, no more responsibility to muster, just me, a shack, and a bottle.

Chapter 4

Drinks for Drunks

(A Field Guide to the Sobriety Wilderness)

I t's not safe outside. The city—any city—is littered with
my drug of choice: from sexy, chic intimidating bars
with clean white lines, Paul Oakenfold beats, minimalist
décor, and even more minimalist hemlines to bars that are
well-worn hole-in-the-walls with sturdy stools, peanuts, and
old-timers who fade like Cheshire cats in and out of the wood
veneers. Bars, pubs, and watering holes blanket the city
like night stars over a dark country prairie. Meanwhile, the
trendy vintners with free wine tastings and shimmering out-
door cafés lurk next to the edgy hair salon, the Vinyasa yoga
studio, or the Whole Foods, eager to pounce once you've been
weakened by the inferiority of your lifestyle compared with
the promise of these merchants of cool (*There, there*, says
the vintner, *your locavore lifestyle and asymmetrical hairdo
are the lies you tell the world; have some truth serum—and*

then have some more). And suddenly you realize that everything is a bar now: the coffee bar, the frozen-yogurt bar, the chocolate bar, the pizza bar—and there is nowhere left to run except straight to the dive liquor store that sells the hard stuff with no bullshit on the side, where the only thing that separates you from feeling normal is a thin brown-paper bag and the time it takes you to walk home.

In other words, you can't just leave the house sober and hope for the best; you have to be armed. Here then is a modest guide to navigating the sloshy, booze-soaked shores of your urban homeland.

Start with a Dinner Party

I wasn't ready to enter a bar and even had strong mixed feelings about most sit-down restaurants. Walking home from work had come to seem like running an alcoholic gauntlet. Mainly, I just stayed home, snug and indoors—practicing my overeating and Internet shopping.

I was feeling self-hating and grumpy at six months sober when Joanna asked me to her house for a dinner party. What better time to take another stab at a social life? I was suffering from such an acute case of cabin fever that I decided to say yes to the invitation instead of squinting my eyes and wondering, *What does she really want from me?* Peter and I set out for Joanna and her husband, Elliot's house with carefully calibrated expectations (*It may be hard, but don't be opposed to having a good time*) and flowers (*When you can't bring a bottle of wine for your host, bring the gift of allergens!*). Still, within moments of our arrival, just after the first awful question had been asked—"What can I get you to drink?"—I came to a sudden and horrible conclusion: People hate alcoholics.

It's not that I expect special treatment. But, if you invite me over for dinner, maybe buy some club soda—or Diet Coke. I don't expect a refrigerator full of hundreds of flavors of Snapple, sodas in every hue, or novelty beverages of all stripes, but *something* other than water would be nice. There was nothing worse than when Joanna turned to her guests with a flourish and listed our options: "We have wine, beer, whiskey, gin-and-tonics, or homemade tequila punch. Sacha, can I get you some water?" She might as well have said, "I have spent hundreds of dollars on exciting beverages for all of my guests but you, Sacha. You, however, may have this lead-based city water I found coming out of the tap in my bathroom sink." Honestly, she wouldn't serve venison to her vegetarian friends, would she? Or let her vegan guest eat the peas while everyone else sank their teeth into prime rib and bacon-infused mashed potatoes?

Already seething, I pulled the baguette and cheese board to my side of the table and gave Joanna's other guests, a schoolteacher and a lawyer, sidelong dirty looks when they reached for a piece. *Don't even think about it. Cheese* is *my cocktail, bitch. Drink your tequila punch and leave me alone!* I ate my bread and water—like a prisoner!—while the others drank their spirits. Little did I know, the worst was yet to come: "Dinner!" sang Joanna from the kitchen. "Coq au vin!" Well, fuck me.

From the other end of the table, Joanna whisper-screamed, "Don't worry, Sach, the alcohol has cooked off," and gave me a wink. Now, in addition to being the dinner-party cheese hoarder, I had to deflect questions about when the baby was due and explain that I am not pregnant, "just a raging alcoholic." There is no better way to silence a room. I heedlessly crammed a forkful of coq au vin into my mouth—and then it happened. Despite all assurances that the alcohol had "cooked off," that my body was not actually ingesting any alcohol, every neuron, synapse, and nerve ending in my brain stood on end and screamed with the full-bodied fervor of the born-again while a thirty-six-member gospel choir somewhere between my ears broke out into song: *I Remember This!*

But while my brain rejoiced, my tongue rebelled. Like a small child first tasting the bitter heat from a cup of coffee, I had no taste for alcohol. While the other guests chatted amiably and cleaned their plates, for me each bite of chicken tasted distinctly pungent. A few months on the wagon and my taste buds had completely reset. Instead of the velvety bite of red-wine sauce, my entire mouth was awash in an odd fermented flavor with hints of vinegar and spoiled grapes. The meal tasted to me as it might to a three-year-old; and, like a three-year-old, I spit the chicken into my napkin—humbly turning my attention back to my bread and water. Alas.

The evening grew dire when dessert was served. "Who wants my famous no-bake amaretto cake?" cooed Joanna, while tears rose to my eyes. No-bake? The alcohol would not have even "cooked off"; this was simply a course I could not have—and, if I was going to relapse, it was not going to be on some sweet inspired by Joanna's latest jaunt down the aisles of Williams-Sonoma. Every part of me yearned to cry, to scream, to beg Joanna to explain to me how she could be so insensitive. *Hey, Joanna,* I telepathically hollered. *Don't serve alcohol to a fucking alcoholic! It's just cruel!* And that's when it occurred to me that Joanna must not like me very much. Perhaps this whole evening was just a scheme to slowly drive me mad. I began to shut down a little then. I felt padlocks clamping down across my soul, walls were erected, defenses deployed—all in an effort to keep the rising alcoholic monster at bay. My anger had awakened a beast and I was craving alcohol now, even that pungent coq au vin sauce. *Give me the pan,* I thought, *I'll lick that shit clean and then guzzle the bottle of cooking wine next to the sink.* And behind a stony façade, I held on tight, squeezing my sobriety until it bled, while a war raged under my skin.

"Who invites an alcoholic over for dinner and prepares every fucking dish with booze?" I later asked Amy. "Tell me! Who does that?"

Amy smiled thoughtfully while she prepared her drink:
She poured a warm can of Diet Pepsi into a Big Gulp cup
brimming with ice; then she pulled lemon wedges wrapped
in napkins out of her purse and squeezed them into the mix
before adding a pinch of Crystal Light, also procured from a
pouch in her purse, and stirred the whole brew with a straw.

"It's like she was intentionally fucking with me," I said.

"It's not about you," Amy replied as she sipped her drink
and waves of caffeinated satisfaction crossed her face.

It's not about you. Fascinating. And as soon as Amy said
it, I knew it was true. Joanna loves to cook, and she finds it
impossible to do so without copious amounts of alcohol. It
simply had nothing to do with me. Indeed, subsequent visits
to Joanna's house have proved that everything she serves is
invariably soaked with alcohol—from her Campari pome-
granate salmon to her Grand Marnier fondue. And yet, I keep
getting invited back. And though this may seem intuitive to
most people, it took me a while to get: I keep getting the invi-
tations because Joanna *likes* me. As it happens, people don't
invite you over—over and over—when they hate you. Fascinating.

Finally, rather than mini-relapse every time I go to
Joanna's, I did something novel: I told the truth.

"I just can't handle the taste of booze—even when the
alcohol has cooked off," I told Joanna as I pushed my penne
pasta à la vodka around in its bowl. It's funny how such a
big issue for me—something that had stormed through my

mind, prompting me to bouts of rage and to make speeches and closing arguments to the demons in my mind—could not have been less of an issue for Joanna herself. "Makes sense," said Joanna. Guess who has never served me alcohol again? People are so much nicer than I think they are.

Now, when I go to a friend's for dinner, I remember not to impose my disease on them. They can drink whatever they like; they don't have to capitulate to my insanity. Also, the truth works far better than wrathful telepathy. Still, I find it doesn't hurt to carry a large purse with mini-bottles of club soda stashed inside—or Diet Pepsi, lemon wedges, and Crystal Light . . .

Next, Try a Cocktail Party

At my first cocktail party in sobriety, I had an epiphany: All that most parties and cocktail hours really are is a bunch of people just *standing there.* I cracked my back, twisting uncomfortably, and slid one foot out of my high-heeled shoe in a semi-orgasmic release before replacing it and repeating with the other foot. Without a drink in my hand, I was not at a reception; I was merely in a crowded room, hovering for an eternity in ill-chosen shoes. And the cocktail hours that precede an event such as, say, a wedding can end up feeling like some yawning expanse, a meaningless pocket of time designed to crush your spirit early so that the rest of the evening—with its mass-produced chicken entrées and droning emcee—will seem tolerable. What's worse, the whole point of the hour, to get people relaxed and chatty before herding them into a charmless catering hall, is not only wasted on me but has the precise opposite effect: Cocktail hours drain my capacity for small talk and leave me exhausted for the main event, during which I am likely to zone out and say something utterly honest like "Is it just me or did that rabbi give you the heebie-jeebies?"

As many workplaces are, my office is fond of holding the occasional cocktail party—a "reward" to the employees that enables the higher-ups to remind everyone that they are still cool and with it and that we are all lucky to work at an office that provides cheese plates and vino in lieu of raises and ergonomic chairs. Sparkling water is rarely passed around on delicate trays at cocktail parties; rather, I often have to fight my way to the bar along with all of the power drinkers—like I used to be—people who can't wait the whole five minutes for the tray of alcohol to pass their way before getting started. Also, I have the distinct disadvantage of having zero social lubricant, which means humoring whoever is talking to me about, say, budget cuts can sometimes take an iron will and accomplished acting—all while trying to snag the one waiter with the elusive club soda. These are the kind of functions I found fairly intolerable even when I did drink and consider downright demented now that I don't. That's why I make a game out of them.

Unwasted

Brush up on your *Harry Potter* and start to think of cocktail parties as Quidditch matches. You are the Seeker. The rented room you are in is the pitch; following the caterer into the kitchen is strictly out of bounds. The club soda is the elusive Golden Snitch. The other people in the room are Bludgers, ready to elbow you out of the game, block access to the Golden Snitch, or, worst of all, engage you in dull conversation in a cruel tactical ploy to keep you from the Snitch altogether. Generally, I find, at most cocktail parties, there is exactly one pre-made club soda over ice. It is hidden on one of the several dozen trays of pinot grigio being circulated throughout the room, and it is your task to locate this lone icy refreshment before the pregnant woman in the crowd does (there is always one). Like *Harry Potter*'s Golden Snitch, the club soda—floating along on its island tray of pinot grigio—darts in and out of the crowd, behind heads and shoulders, dips and bobs, weaves and swoops in a maddening dance while you try to swipe at it without drawing unnecessary attention to yourself. You get one point for each club soda you can drink before you have to pee.

I am never so thirsty as when I cannot find a drink. Cocktail parties are kind of like being trapped on a lifeboat on the ocean, surrounded by water with nary a drop to drink. With their endless jibber-jabbering and small talk, they not only induce a kind of ferocity of thirst I've never before known, they also make me yearn for something, anything, to occupy my hands and mouth. A tiny over-iced sparkling water with a Lilliputian straw that is drained through osmosis the second my lips touch the sides will do. I just need something that allows me to feel like, in some small way, I am normal, that I am participating in the normal course of things, that I am acknowledging the time-honored ritual of imbibing liquids while discussing the weather ("Hot, right? I mean I need a shower just from walking to the bus stop"), that I am no heretic, no outlier, no fundamentalist, that I am capable of carrying the totemic glass and damp napkin without devolving into an incomprehensible alcoholic panic.

I also find it amusing to watch the young kids at the office during a cocktail party—the interns, the assistants, the newbies. They gleefully snap up delicate wineglasses like they were two-for-one Miller Lites at the campus pub. They throw back pinot noir as though it were indistinguishable from the novelty beverages of their clan: Malibu coconut rum floats, Mike's Hard Lemonade, Captain Morgan, Jägermeister shots, Long Island iced teas, Red Bull and vodka, and kamikazes. The liquor companies have pulled off the neat trick of making a perfectly legal and accessible substance subversive and cool. And now I get to watch as the Barely Legals leave their perches at the little kids' table and join the adults at the big one. They can barely contain their excitement as they beam and think: *I am like totally drinking at work right now!* And then there is that kid at the office who sneers at his own peers while he channels Holden Caulfield; he swirls and ostentatiously sniffs his wine for the better part of an hour until it is sheer foam, and all I can think is, *Stop! I may not drink the stuff anymore, but I won't stand for it being abused like that. My God, kid, what are you doing, some kind of inane molecular gastronomy experiment?*

The Barely Legals make me feel normal. With their insecurities and overcompensations, their swirling and chugging and beaming, I can feel more like an adult, more like I belong. I am not as awkward as they are; I am more of a grown-up. I blend. Just another ordinary adult playing a mental game of Quidditch against the pregnant lady.

Advanced Outing: The Happy Hour

Has there ever been a more contrived hour than the "happy" hour? Has any moment in life ever been so sculpted, so artificially imposed over the template of a daily life? I have always opposed the stinging reality implied by the happy hour: that the precious sixty minutes between the tedium of one's job and the oppression of one's household is in fact a Happy Hour, that the rest of the day is composed of frustrating hours and boring hours and depressing hours, but—lo!—the Happy Hour swoops in at five o'clock on Friday and whispers, *Punch out, sweetheart, cheap rail drinks and sweaty men in loosened neckties await.* What does that say about life if people everywhere need to carve out a special time in order to make the rest of the week tolerable? What does it say that happiness is defined by a human mass of repressed adolescent urges and collegiate nostalgia pouring into dark crowded rooms for artichoke dip and light beer?

Though a "happy" hour is supposedly a fun event after-hours that you theoretically have free will over whether or not to attend, I have found them to be maddeningly mandatory. I have been exhorted by countless colleagues and bosses alike to "Come on! Join the fun! We'll just stop by for a minute . . ." And, exhortations aside, many of those happy hours are savvy networking events it might actually behoove me to attend. Once at the happy hour, however, I am always tense. And, in early sobriety, I was practically frozen.

"Sacha's here!" yells Tom over the din of Top 40 tunes and the disembodied laughter and squawking of a few hundred people decked out in Ann Taylor and Brooks Brothers as I squeeze into the bar. "Dude, you never come out anymore!"

I am in the lions' den, surrounded by a circus of liquor. I used to be the ringleader. Now I feel like an imposter, scared I'll be "made" and summarily kicked out for being so square.

"I am totally buying you a beer," says Tom. "How about a shot?"

"No thanks, I've had enough," I say.

"What?" asks Tom.

"I'll have a club soda with lime," I say. "See if you can keep up."

Tom orders a Dogfish Head 60 Minute India Pale Ale, a

beer I have never heard of before, and I get a little wistful. There are so many new drinks out there now that I have never tried and, God willing, never will. And yet, I can't help but pine for that new perfect drink I have never known. It's like when Jerry Garcia died, and I thought, *But I've never been to a Grateful Dead show!* I've also never bought a Grateful Dead album or listened to them in earnest at all, but once the opportunity was gone, I could not help but have regret. *The leader of the most important live band in history has died, and I never saw him perform; why is this happening to me?*

I realize Tom has been talking for a while now as I have been contemplating his trendy microbrew.

"So I'm like, 'If you're going to give me shit about taking time off, then maybe you shouldn't take four fucking weeks off.' You know?"

I am in a sea of booze and resentments. This is the *raison d'être* of the happy hour: to blow off steam about the boss, flash your teeth at your coworkers, and guzzle liquid courage to fuel your hubris before going home.

I have to leave.

And leaving is a tricky business. It is important, whether at a happy hour or at a party, to have a solid exit strategy ahead of time. I find that, as I wander through any happy hour or party, there is a moment where I realize that I have been there an acceptable amount of time, that, indeed, I wouldn't even be the first to leave. The problem is: The very instant I think this, I'm done; I have to leave right then, that second. The second it occurs to me that I can leave, all of the psychic energy is drained from me. I lose the ability to speak nicely, to nod appreciatively, to even attempt a pretext at interest. The moment the possibility of leaving arises, I must be free. I must have air. I must be on the street in front of the building breathing cool, uncrowded air and taking one step after another in the direction of my own living room.

At happy hours I can at least be vague.

"Tom!" I say. "I just remembered I don't feel well. I know, weird, right? So I'll see you Monday."

I then ease my way out past the clunky designer purses bobbing along on the tide of people lapping against the bar front, past the precariously perched pitchers of beer, and past the huddle of young men smoking just outside the door, their collars turned up against the chilly evening. "Going so soon?" calls one. I don't look to see who it is; I don't look back; I don't respond. I don't have any business being here.

But parties with friends require a much more nuanced exit strategy and a deft handling of Peter. It's not that I don't love my friends; I adore them. At Jake's birthday party, for example, I had a lot of fun for a long time. I listened to Julianna go through a point-by-point takedown of Twitter ("I'm not going to *follow* you. I'm not a *follower*"), bonded with Ruth over writing with a full-time job ("Here's to no vacations!"), and laughed with Jake's plan to get rich off of Peter's nuclear nonproliferation expertise ("We'll advise Hollywood, dude, and make a fortune. I'm serious!"). But then I start to hear my friends' slightly slurred words, I focus on what I can't have, I get cranky, and, as fast as the thought occurs to me, I am desperate to leave.

Unfortunately, leaving is generally a multistage process that can take a good half an hour—if you're lucky. The mission is to find the host as quickly as possible to say good-bye. However, Peter is quick to point out all the other people at the party he'd like to say good-bye to as well ("Okay, I just want to see Manisha and then say good-bye to Christopher and Lea—oh!—and I have to remind Kevin about breakfast next week"). I, myself, no longer really care about saying good-bye to anyone, but will make an effort to at least find Jake while Peter has parting mini-conversations with half a dozen other people. And that's when I realize that Jake is in the kitchen while I am at the front door. This means I have to navigate the endless stretch of living room and hallway that have expanded before me like some kind of twisted funhouse prank. Suddenly the two-bedroom apartment in Dupont Circle is fucking Versailles, and making my way from one end to the other without getting waylaid by semi-familiar faces and well-intentioned pleasantries is something akin to *Logan's Run*.

"Sacha, what are you working on these days?" asks Toby, a writer friend who has a nasty habit of offering unsolicited advice—"I'm not sure that's your color, doll"—appearing out of nowhere by my side.

And that is when, instead of admitting that I'm on my way out, as though I fear Toby will judge me and then tackle me to the floor before letting me leave, I make a rookie mistake: "I'm going to go get a drink, can I get you one?"

Fuck. Now I have to play waitress before I can leave. Which means I have to go to the kitchen, get the drinks, deliver the drinks to Toby, doubtless endure some commentary on Toby's latest success compared with mine, go back to the kitchen, say good-bye to Jake, and then make my way back to the front door. And find Peter.

I used to think of conversation as a competition. Instead of listening to your end of the conversation, I would be plotting my own response in advance. I would spar with earnest folks who were just trying to connect with me, and I would think up dazzling, killer barbs sure to amuse and shock them. I would not listen so much as grab small pieces of what they said that I could then mold into a platform for what I wanted to say all along. I could win any conversation.

Now, as I darted through a labyrinthine corridor to find Jake, I could hear Amy's voice inside my head: *It's not about you.*

"It really means a lot to me that you and Peter came tonight," says Jake as I corner him and his girlfriend, Lexa, in the kitchen. I suppress the instinct to retort, to subvert his sincerity (*You don't have to hide it anymore; I know you're gay for Peter*).

"You're one of my favorites, dude," I say with full eye

contact. "We love you. Happy birthday. And stop staring at Peter's ass." Progress!

By the time I lure Peter away from a riveting discussion of the new nuclear-arms reduction treaty (only in D.C., I swear), I am frantic with the desire to leave. I am ready to claw at the curtains and leap to the sidewalk.

Now I prepare an exit strategy before every event I attend. I give Peter a subtle hand signal (usually my finger dragged across my throat while my tongue lolls to one side) and then we have twenty minutes to wrap things up. If people are not said good-bye to within that time, we e-mail them later. I leave home with Perrier in my purse, scope out the exits of the party, put Amy on speed dial, and listen when I am spoken to. It's not safe outside. You just can't be too careful.

Final Exam: Holidays and Other Family Functions

No matter how newly sober and irritable you are, your family is still bound to insist on the pleasure of your company. And, if you are really lucky—as Peter and I are—your families will also live within forty-five minutes of each other and insist on meeting.

At first, it seemed convenient that Peter's Manhattan-based parents built their country house in the Columbia County farmlands outside of Albany. My father, stepmother, and sister lived in the countryside near Albany all-year-round themselves. And my mother is an easy train ride away, due west of Albany in Syracuse. Peter and I imagined holidays in which we would set out from Washington, coast right past the traffic, circumvent the tricky ins and outs of negotiating Manhattan, head straight for God's country, and spend a lot less time crisscrossing New York State. And, while the New Jersey Turnpike routinely cures us of such heady thoughts, once arrived in the greater Albany area, there is something easy and convenient about being able to shoot between one set of parents and another. And then Peter's folks invited my dad and crew over for lunch.

"There are just two topics you should probably avoid while we are there, Dad," I say to my father on the ride over to Peter's family's house. "Religion and politics." My step-mother, Deb, listens carefully as I lean over from the back-seat; she is aware that my father is only half-listening himself as he hurls the minivan (a minivan that is liberally covered in progressive bumper stickers) down back-country roads at eighty miles an hour while my nine-year-old sister, Shiloh, and I swing back and forth in our seats like rag dolls with every death-defying curve.

"You don't have to worry about me," says my father, as Deb and I exchange a look.

"No, I know, Dad," I say. "It's just that Peter's father is pretty religious."

"I'm not going to offend anybody's religion," says my father, a little taken aback.

"No, of course not!" I say. My father is not some hardcore nonbeliever; indeed, he has a very real spiritual streak. Any given month, he is as likely to be reading about Jewish intellectual history as Sufi mysticism. Of course, that particular month, he had just read, heh heh, Richard Dawkins's atheist manifesto, *The God Delusion*.

"How religious?" asks my father.

"Like, he goes to church several times a week," I say.

"Several times a week?!" gasps my father, and I cannot tell if he is feigning horror to mock my concern or if he is actually startled.

"Also," I say, and this is the real bombshell given the delight my father has taken in talking politics with Peter, "he's conservative. He's *a* conservative. He's a conservative Republican."

"Oh yeah?" says my father. "Conservative, huh?"

"Like, he definitely voted for George W. Bush," I say. "In 2004."

"But Peter—"

"They have their differences," I blurt out quickly, all too aware of the myriad ways any conversation involving my father, Peter, and Peter's father could go very wrong.

"Alright, alright, I got it," says my father, no doubt annoyed that I feel I must prep him for this interaction.

Deb shoots me a smile that says, *Hey, you told him what you had to tell him. What will be will be.*

Once at Peter's family's house, a place they spent years planning and building to be the ultimate modern country hideaway, introductions are made and, before I know it, we are all sitting quietly around the dining room table. Predictably enough, lunch with the parents is a little awkward, and I am very aware of just how nice a stiff drink would taste right now. Peter and I definitely take on the heavy lifting, telling stories about our jobs and lives in D.C., but overall there are plenty of pregnant pauses hanging in the air. Maybe it is to fill the silence, or maybe because his subconscious could think of nothing else after my admonitions in the minivan, or maybe because Peter has just told a work story about *The New Republic* (which my dad reads regularly, which he alternately heralds or screams at, and which had recently reviewed the Dawkins book), but my father says:

"Isn't it just awful how much George Bush invokes God when he speaks?"

It is, in its own way, a kind of brilliant twofer. In one fell swoop, my father has simultaneously staked both sacred cows I have asked him to steer clear of. What's more, it is perfectly obvious that he has no idea at all that he has said anything provocative in the slightest as he looks brightly and expectantly at Peter (who is busy squeezing the life force out of my thigh and picking his jaw up off the table). But I wear a huge smile on my face. Now that the "worst" has happened,

86

now that my father has, in his own impervious way, brought up the very two topics I have asked him to circumnavigate, I feel silly for ever having asked him not to do so. Not only does my father have a kind of distracted-philosophy-professor way about him that precludes too much predictability—as he is likely to voice any given thought he has any given moment he has it—but it is exactly this quality that makes him such a great conversationalist. Looking at my father across the table as the carefully constructed pointers I'd given him lie in wreckage around us, I beam. I've never loved him more. And maybe a little part of me knows, this is exactly the sort of thing I do all the time. Of course, that is when Peter's father's voice interrupts my thoughts.

"How so?" asks Peter's father from the head of the table.

And, before my father can deliver a short disquisition on the separation of church and state and how God has not personally given George W. Bush a foreign-policy blueprint, Peter takes a slug of wine with one hand while still inflicting bruises on my leg with the other, and says too loudly, "How about a tour of the house?!"

As I try to imagine what Peter's father thinks of my commie-pinko tribe (I might as well get used to it, I figure; my mother arrives for her own visit in two days—fresh from her retirement gig at Peace Action of Central New York), we all stand for a tour of the house—including a peek at the master bedroom in which a large crucifix is prominently displayed. Later, when I say to Peter's father, "Well, the cat's out of the bag! I come from liberal stock," he leans in and says in his unwaveringly gracious manner, "That's what keeps the conversation interesting."

Still, I cannot shake the fear that any familial discussion can and will veer wildly out of control if I am not there to help nudge and steer it back on course. When I feel tension between members of Peter's family or my own, I immediately revert back to a time before my dad's new family, before my mom's new big life, when I was the only-child of soon-to-be divorced parents with no one of my rank in the family, no one but pet cats and teddy bears in my room while my folks argued downstairs. And, even as I am aware of the cliché I have become, I crave a drink like nobody's business when I think there's a chance a family moment might go wrong—as when Peter and his brother disagree, when my mother asks me for the fifth time if I'm sure I'm fine, when Peter's mom frets over which serving bowls to use, and, yes, when my father says something overtly liberal or Peter's father says something overtly conservative. Because, when I feel order slipping through my fingers, I get scared. I know how easy it could be for me to slink right back into chaos.

I have found that surrounding myself by so many parents at such a stressful time as the holidays is not without serious risks to my fragile mental state. That's why I've taken to smoking imaginary pot. When I hear the maternal worry that perfection of the family meal is not a guarantee or the sibling squabbling so unfamiliar to my only child's ear, I clasp thumb to forefinger, lift a fake joint to my lips, and deeply inhale. I was never much of a pot fan, always preferring alcohol, but something about channeling my inner surfer dude totally relaxes me. Where other relatives can down half a bottle of sherry before the turkey is done to relieve their angst, I can smoke imaginary pot and zen out, man. It works on the Jersey Turnpike, too.

Number 4 on the Sacha Fantasy Relapse Pass: Saving the World from Nuclear Holocaust

It is 1986; a frigid breeze cuts across the Icelandic shore. Mikhail Gorbachev looks hale; his port-wine birthmark especially ruddy in the cold October air. Port. Wine. I have had neither a glass of port nor wine in months. A rich, velvety cabernet would be just the thing on such an icy day, too—warming the belly as the fire is stoked and some baked brie and fig jam is passed around. Alas, I have more important matters to attend to at this summit.

For the past few years, I have been advising President Ronald Reagan on issues of arms control. Though nothing I have ever said has been as effective as a late-night viewing of The Day After *over a bowl of Jelly-Bellys, I still try. My latest ideological battle has been to convince Reagan that the Strategic Defense Initiative isn't worth*

*fighting for in arms-reduction talks with the Soviets. Af-
ter all, I argued, if there are no nuclear weapons, there is
no need to defend against them. But Reagan is fond of the
so-called Star Wars program, imagining laser skirmishes
in deep space. "It's certainly a clever nickname, sir," I
said to him yesterday. "Perhaps we could use it somewhere else? I bet the air force would love to be known as
Star Warriors . . ." That seemed to do the trick. For the
last twenty-four hours, I had hammered out the details of
the most comprehensive nuclear de-escalation in the history of the world. And now I am in Reykjavik, watching
as the two men who will end the nuclear era altogether
shake hands.*

*"A cold setting to end the Cold War!" Gorbachev ex-
claims as he claps a beaming Reagan on the back. Despite the plummeting temperature, the Russians open a
chilled bottle of Stolichnaya. (What the hell do Icelanders
drink? I wonder.) A mist spirals out of the bottle's neck,
creating a kind of alcoholic apparition; a chill runs up
my spine. I can hear the wisdom of alcoholics past, their
spectral whisperings swirling from the vodka: Nothing is
more important than your sobriety.*

A small glass of the frigid Stoli is handed to me.

*Gorbachev exclaims, "To total nuclear disarmament
and world peace!" as he and the Russian contingent
throw back the shots.*

"To world peace!" says Reagan, grinning. He swal-

lows the liquor and does a sort of cough-chuckle before saying, "I've been waiting for this ever since I saw The Day After.*"*

I find myself a bit teary, aware of the weight of history all around me, thinking of the books that will document this very moment, the moment a small band of earnest foreign policy strategists saved the world from itself. I begin to brainstorm titles for the memoir I will surely write: Nuclear Freeze: No, Really, It's Cold in Reykjavik! *or, perhaps,* You're Welcome, Earth: My Role in Securing Your Future. *But that is when I notice that everyone in the room is looking at me.*

"It would be a nice gesture if everyone drank the vodka," Gorbachev says meaningfully to Reagan while gesturing toward me with raised eyebrows. "I would not agree to total nuclear disarmament if I thought any one of you had reservations."

"Scoblic! Drink the damn vodka," hisses my commander-in-chief out of the side of his mouth.

Nothing is more important than your sobriety. Really? Nothing?

I smile as I raise my glass: "To world peace, gentlemen!"

Chapter 5

Escape from Bitch Mountain

"**D**o you not LOVE it here?!" squealed Sophie on my first day at *The New Republic*. "Sometimes I just want to sing! *The New Republic, ooh la la, fact-check here, copy-edit there, la la la.* And we have so many cute boys! Eek! But wait," she continued, holding up the pages of a piece she was editing by a famous evolutionary biologist. "Have you ever really pondered the *nature* of nature versus nurture? I've been thinking about it a lot lately and it's blowing my mind! Oh! I am going to the Black Cat tonight to hear Bebel Gilberto and review it for the *City Paper*—you should totally come with. Omigod! Then I have to finish my piece on new-new-new-wave feminism. Ack! So much to do! So excited you are here! Do you listen to Belle and Sebastian?"

"Will working here make me feel like you do?" I asked. It would not. But then, really, what would? Sophie was the exuberant drummer for a local band but could easily have been the lead singer; she brought her parents to see her perform in rock shows, hosted BYOH parties (Bring Your Own Haiku), danced in her chair while she edited, read everything she could get her hands on, and went out every night of the week. Her mind is like an ultra-high-speed kaleidoscope, swirling together color and information and totems and tidbits into wild blends while reflecting light and radiance on whoever is fortunate enough to be listening. Most of the time when I was drinking, I found it a bit much.

Sophie's infinite internal pool of gratefulness ("It's soooo beautiful outside!"; "You MUST taste this!"; "Look, there's Mason! Don't you just love Mason? We are so lucky to know him") conflicted with my own internal victim and natural defensiveness ("I'm not thin enough for nice weather yet"; "I love how we find a good lunch spot and it's closing next week"; "Fucking Mason, always walking around"). I also watched as Sophie would have a couple of cocktails and then happily switch to Coke.

I had been to this dance before. I'd meet someone new and go out for drinks only to find they would just, well, stop. Stop?! We were out for fucking drinks after all! And that was it for me: No matter how much I had liked this person just moments before and no matter how much we had in common, I would begin to mentally erase her from my mind. To me, it was obvious that we just weren't going to make it. She might as well have told me she admired Hitler, because the two-drink drinker was never going to be a steady pal of mine.

But Sophie was irrepressible. She didn't care if I continued to drink, she just wanted to stay out and go to a concert or go to a club or go to a play or play the jukebox or play pool or play charades or play an instrument or learn an instrument or learn a foreign language or apply for a Fulbright because . . . because . . . Because why not? I was charmed and scared. Despite her lifestyle's apparent compatibility with my own, Sophie's lust for life scared the ever-loving shit out of me.

And so I rejected the normal folks—the two-drink drinkers—with their "early morning meetings" and "responsibilities" for hipper, cooler friends. And, when the cool friends, like Sophie, weren't as serious about doing the lonely work of drinking as I'd hoped, I moved on to sketchier, shadier friends. And, when the sketchy, shady friends made my skin crawl, I always had Tessa and Jack. Two perfect friends who had the unique ability to be both wonderful people *and* big drinkers. This was a rare combination—something I had learned firsthand a year before in journalism school: More often than not, the big drinkers are way less cool than the two-drink drinkers. Before I ever started at *The New Republic*, I had left D.C. for a year to get my graduate degree. At the time, I even thought of it as an opportunity to detox a little, to renew.

I entered graduate school with a sense of purpose. New town, new goals, new life. I decided I would swear off friends altogether. I didn't think I had a drinking problem so much as a good-times problem. I had no self-control in the face of a good time. And so, I decided that I didn't need companionship; I just needed to kick ass in school. That lasted until the first wine-and-cheese orientation reception. Upon meeting my fellow magazine journalism classmates—a profession that would start to gasp its last breaths just as we all would finish our first years as editorial assistants at insolvent magazines and realize that we had made a crucial error in career judgment—I became convinced that I had nothing to fear from these intellectual mediocrities, these babies straight from college, that I would not have to work as hard as I'd thought, and that I should start drinking as much as possible as soon as possible.

Besides, I had already made a friend: Kirstin. Well, we were friends in high school and I hadn't seen her since, but here she was in my graduate program. I remembered Kirstin as up for anything, ready to party with older guys, leave the house at eleven on a school night, and say with a breezy detachment the kind of things that would have been high treason in my house during high school, like: "I'm not sure I'm going to college; I might move to India and live on an *ashram* for a while." But Graduate School Kirstin was a new Kirstin, every bit as impressive but suddenly grounded, happier, and more beautiful than I remembered. Now she was a yoga teacher, a poet, wildly curious, and completely uninterested in parties; she was more likely to want to take a long walk and talk, go swimming, or just go to the movies—a fully participatory event marked by Kir's constant questions and complete inability to whisper: "Now where the fuck did that guy come from?" she'd ask the screen in a completely audible speaking voice, or, "Sach, you have to explain this to me. That's the brother, right?" She was experiential where I was escapist. Kirstin knew herself, and her confidence was intoxicating. Were we each to get a bad haircut, Kirstin would immediately reproach the hairdresser, demand a fix, leave looking fantastic, and only pay half; I would say my haircut was fine, overtip, go home, try to fix it myself, and then wear a hat for the next month.

Despite my sense of Kirstin as the bad girl in high school, it was pretty clear now that Kirstin was someone you could take home to Mom, and Mom would be pleased, and Mom would know you were hanging out with a good crowd. Kirstin didn't look like she'd been up all night, she didn't have the odor of crushed cigarettes clinging to her, and she didn't seem uncomfortable talking to people's parents. She was a freshly scrubbed, tan, smart woman who was on a much easier path than I. Kirstin seemed to have earned her serenity—perhaps her wild high school days had left her unimpressed with the dark corners of adulthood I found so thrilling—and she had an easy handle on honesty, a concept I was still hazy on.

Which is probably why I ditched her for Vera. After a few weeks of school, Vera invited me over for drinks with some other students. Vera was a tall young woman at five-foot-ten, a voluptuous, Eurasian, dark beauty and somehow powerful. I felt unworthy in her presence as she glided through crowds topping off glasses of cheap merlot as though we were on Park Avenue and not in upstate New York. She wore expensive clothes, drank only red wine (usually several bottles in a night), spoke a little Japanese (a gift from her mother's side of the family), and seemed not to care a wit about school except as a vehicle for her own popularity—an odd thing, I thought, for a grad student to care about. She threw the best parties, knew students from every graduate program, and slept with the teaching assistant in her graphic-design course (a sexy spiky-haired hipster who threw her an A at the end of the semester and once told me she passed out nearly every time they had sex). I liked her right away.

And she seemed to know me on spec. "I was wondering when you were going to stop hanging out with those blondes," she said, referring to Kirstin and another woman I had studied with that semester, as she ushered me through her apartment (a rental she had painted deep shades of gray and mauve) and handed me a glass of wine. In the kitchen, Vera's roommate, an anemic and sour-looking law student named Lori, was frying plantains apparently as an appetizer. "She lived in Honduras for a summer, so now she's insisting on making Latin American specialties. Honestly, what is so exotic about putting bananas in a pan?" Vera whispered as we approached the stove. Lori offered me a freshly charred plantain. "I'm just not a huge fan of plantains," I demurred in what I hoped was a nice voice. Lori looked as though she were being forced to slave away in the kitchen, but it was obvious to me that Vera wanted nothing more than for Lori to take her sad-sack self anywhere but Vera's glamorous cocktail party. "Sacha hates plantains," Vera hissed to Lori as she pulled me into the next room. "There's some people I want you to meet in here, princess." She smiled at me and gave my arm a squeeze. The attention was intoxicating, her ruthlessness mesmerizing.

We were inseparable for quite a while after that. We drank together almost every night, many of which started with an elaborate ritual in which we sipped wine while applying makeup and singing Erykah Badu. We skipped the college bars and headed downtown; we smoked cigars; we made out with dudes and then laughed behind their backs; we made going to the movies an event to be buttressed first by cocktails and then by an after party. And early on, there were warning signs that perhaps Vera wasn't as awesome as she seemed. She told me that her last year of college was marked by a severe addiction to heroin ("I was so thin. I've never looked better!") and that she quit cold turkey with a few weeks of R & R at her folks' house in the country ("They thought I had mono!"), a carelessly told story I wasn't sure I believed. Naturally, the heroin didn't bother me, but the nagging sense that this was a carefully constructed lie designed to make her appear mysterious and reckless did. She told me she won her massive cherry-red Ford Explorer in a contest:

Daughter of the Year. And I thought, *Okay, she's spoiled.* But I still let her pick me up for class every day ("Hop in, princess!"). "I'm very capricious about my boyfriends," she said blithely after I asked after her spiky-haired graphic-design teaching assistant. And when I wondered if I looked nice in my outfit, she reassured me by saying, "I'm a very shallow person, Sacha. If you weren't attractive, I wouldn't be hanging out with you." I laughed it off at the time as a joke, but later could only think of the expression: "When people show you who they are, believe them."

Yet I basked in Vera's attention, drank with her, and tried to make her laugh. And I assiduously ignored her front teeth, which seemed to get darker with every sip of merlot—like some kind of night creature revealing its true nature the longer the evening wore on; her entire mouth was ultimately a gaping morass of purple, a wine monster who'd throw you under the bus for another stem-less glass of Sutter Home.

"What's on your mind, princess?" Vera asked as she offered me a brownie from a carton bearing a Post-it Note labeled "Lori's."

"I'm just wicked hung-ovah," I said. *Wicked* had become my new favorite word ever since I heard I'd be covering the 2000 presidential primaries in New Hampshire (New Hampsha) that February for my political-reporting class. I planned on fully assimilating. But I couldn't discuss going to New

Hampshire with Vera ("Okay, okay, okay, no shoptalk; it's the weekend," she'd admonish after I brought up politics on a Wednesday night). And anyway, as the cool nights and warm days of September drew to an end, it seemed silly to care about Vera's exasperations with a trip still so far off.

We split a bottle of red before heading downtown, blasting Biggie Smalls and smoking cigarettes in the Explorer before ditching it in a parking lot for the night. At the first bar, a band we knew was playing, and Vera and I sang along while throwing back wine like water and doing shots. In the bathroom, Vera looked at me critically. "Get that thing off your head," she said. I was wearing a black, elastic headband in my hair, with a few bangs escaping—fetchingly, I thought—from its grasp. "What is this? The 1980s?" She scowled, forcefully yanking my hair and grabbing the headband from my head—not a difficult task for Vera, who towered over me. There was a lot to think about in that moment. I was hurt, of course, that my choice in headgear was so openly attacked. I feared, too, that the attack was on the mark—that I had been going out in public with this dated homage to Madonna on my head like a silly teenage wannabe. I felt shamed for my terrible taste. I was angry, naturally, that I would allow someone to be so rude to me. And I was embarrassed; who else was listening? But a glance in the mirror told me I didn't have to think too deeply on Vera's cruelty; the elastic band had already forged a deep line across my mane, every hair jutting out at right angles just above my brow. In the absence of a shower, the headband was going back on—stylish or not.

Vera rolled her eyes at me as I clutched for it. I thought for a second she might hold it out of reach, that she might actually use her size to thwart me. I imagined fighting for my headband, tussling in the bathroom like a grade-schooler—though I never had actually tussled in bathrooms in grade school. I imagined her laughing as I vainly leapt at her for my limp elastic headband. But instead she let me take it from her and said, "Let's get out of here."

The next bar doubled as a coffee shop during the day; its walls were lined with mugs, french presses, and travel cups. Vera grabbed a set of small espresso cups and quickly deposited one into each of our purses with a sly wink. Again I was taken back to grade school, where a five-finger discount was a mark of coolness—and again I had never been a true shoplifter: Preferring lying to thievery, I'd brag about all of my stolen albums and rubber bangle bracelets after first paying for them all in full. "This is why the prices here are so high," I joked to Vera. "They always have to buy new cups." Though my social-costs argument seemed lost on her, Vera promptly grabbed the cup from my bag and added it to her own. "I want the complete set," she explained. But it seemed to me the repossession of the stolen cup meant more: I was no longer her partner in crime; we were no longer in this night together.

Unwasted

After a waiter whom Vera was friendly with comped us our drinks, she grabbed my wrist and smiled. It was clear she'd just had a very bad idea. I drained my glass, and the two of us followed the waiter's path from our table through a pair of swinging doors and into the kitchen. Before any of the employees even noticed us under the unfairly harsh fluorescent lighting—two drunk women teetering inside the doorway; one with a dated headband—Vera pulled me into a walk-in fridge to our right. I sensed this was not her first time in this bar's kitchen. "Did you used to work here or something?" I asked as she shushed me and filled her cradled arms with eggs. "Grab some!" she shrieked, and I remember thinking, *Is this the sort of thing I do? Is this wild and silly and funny?* I was so drunk, I could no longer remember what my lines in the sand were, or if I even had any.

We stumbled back into the anonymous dark of the bar and headed for the door, each of us dropping several eggs as we shuffled through the crowd. I was vaguely aware of a man shouting at us from the back; I think he was trying to stop us—from stealing eggs? It hardly seemed worth it. And it didn't matter, soon I'd be outside, and the freedom of that thought beckoned. I didn't want any eggs. I didn't want to be near Vera. I just wanted the cool rush of the outdoors on my face. Once through the bar's main entrance I ran down the block and discreetly dropped the three eggs I had left in a gutter drain. Breathless, I looked back to see Vera hurling her eggs at the façade of the bar and screaming with laughter. I approached her—"Vera, we've got to go!"—tugging on her jacket. To which, she promptly egged me.

Moments after I turned on my heel and walked away from Vera, she was at my side—along with the waiter from the bar. "Don't be so mad, princess," she purred. "Max is going to drive us home." My eighties headband askew, blouse egged, and the onset of the spins just starting, I let Vera guide me to Max the Waiter's car.

I'm going to have to really think about tonight, I said to myself as we pulled up to my apartment—aware that some lesson was pending, some wisdom could be divined from this debacle. If only I could sharpen my focus. I stumbled out of the car and started to wave good-bye only to find Vera had leapt out of the car herself and was skipping over to a set of plastic lawn chairs on my building's front yard. It was the kind of college-town neighborhood in which beautiful but run-down, large, old Victorian homes were subdivided into units with used couches stationed on the front porches and Christmas lights ablaze all year long. Vera leaned back in her lawn chair, lit a cigarette, and gazed up at the stars. Max the Waiter stood next to his car, unsure why this drop-off had turned into a layover.

"I'm going to bed," I slurred, walking past Vera. As far as I was concerned she could lounge in the front yard all night. She ignored me as I climbed the steps to the porch, opened the screen door, and started to root around in my purse. And then she said, "Don't you need these?" and held out a set of keys. Oh, fuck.

She had retrieved the purloined espresso cup from my purse and stolen my keys. That felt like hours ago. Good Lord, what if I hadn't taken the ride home with her and Max?

"Give me the keys, Vera," I said, approaching the lawn chair. "I'm done."

I stood stiffly next to the lawn chair and glared at her, but she just grabbed me around the waist and dangled the keys from the fingertips of her far hand—all while I flashed back to the bar bathroom earlier that night, when I was certain she was going to make me, the shortie, jump for my head-band. Apparently, she just needed more wine to get there.

"Aww, princess," she said as she tried to pull me down to her lap. But the lawn chair gave out and both Vera and I were sent sprawling. "Whoa, there," said Max the Waiter from far away, a note of concern in his voice. Off to the right, Vera was laughing uncontrollably. I stayed still, my head on the soft ground, and watched through blades of dewy grass as the lights came on in the house across the street. *Maybe the neighbors will yell at us,* I thought. *Maybe they'll threaten to call the cops and Vera will leave.*

"Priiin-cesssss!" she yelled. For the first time, it occurred to me that this was a weird nickname. I bet her parents—the Ford Explorer-gifting parents—called her "princess" to make her feel special. Vera clambered on top of me in a tangle of limbs and earth while I twisted beneath her. "Get her off of me," I yelled to Max the Waiter while Vera continued to laugh. But Vera pinned me to the ground, using all of her weight against me.

I've been very lucky. I was never really bullied; I have always been well-liked. And I, in turn, liked everybody. I happily hung out on the math team in high school and just as happily threw back beers in the parking lot before school dances with the cool kids. But now, I thought, perhaps the lack of bullying wasn't because *I* was so nice; perhaps I was just tracked into the cool cliques by dint of the right clothes and looks. Perhaps in a parallel universe unfairly short Sacha routinely had big kids sit on top of her while she pleaded for her keys. This had, after all, happened to me once before—at camp. At camp, nobody cared about your cliques back home. At camp, we were all tabula rasa, eleven-year-olds in practical shorts and pigtails hoping to be ascribed the characteristics of cool: the top-level swim group, a facility with making plastic-lace macramé bracelets, and a healthy stoicism in the face of campfire ghost stories. And, at camp, I had once been pinned down by bigger girls who wrestled off my limp and utterly unnecessary training bra before running it up the flagpole.

I remembered this now at age twenty-six as Vera threatened to spit in my face. "I'll do it," she goaded. I couldn't fathom the threat. Did she want something in return for not spitting in my face? I mean, I wasn't the one holding *her* keys hostage.

Perhaps out of boredom, perhaps concern, Max the Waiter was suddenly hovering above us. "Okay," he said. "Time to go." And he pulled a still-snickering Vera off me as easily as she pulled me down.

"Check ya later, princess," said Vera while she casually tossed my keys into the bushes. And it was clear she felt that she had done nothing wrong, that she was just having some naughty fun with her little princess toy.

I crawled over to the bushes in a haze, searching for the house keys. I was acutely aware that, were a friend (a true friend) in my position right now—egged, sore, muddy, and clawing through a thicket for house keys—I'd firmly advise that friend to kick Vera's ass to the curb. Just as, when I dated the guy who wanted to keep "us" a secret, I knew I'd never let a good pal stay in that relationship. Why wasn't I taking advice I would self-righteously and even indignantly extol to others? More important: Why are the most toxic people in my life always the biggest drinkers? Just as Vera was more playmate than trusted confidante, my "secret" boyfriend was more drinking buddy than loving companion. But I wasn't ready to think about that particular quandary just yet.

The next week at school, I broke it off with Vera. I told her I didn't think we worked well together. In the moment, she was elegant; she agreed that we weren't a good match as friends and even wished me the best. But then, one day over pizza, a fellow classmate asked me, "So I heard you stole Vera's keys?" while I tried to process the mind-fuck being laid down on me. The next time I saw her out, Vera was with some students from the law school, including the guy who played Dave Matthews songs on his guitar all day on the quad and a little hipster chick with charcoal eyes and a dark bob. "Hey princess!" Vera said, hugging the hipster chick; I couldn't help but notice she was my height.

I ran back to Kirstin, certain she would judge me, certain I would have to earn her friendship, certain that she would say, "Well, look who needs a friend now." But that's the funny thing about kind people; Kirstin just seemed pleased to have my company. As her sense of self-worth had nothing to do with whether or not the great Sacha rolled through, it had never even crossed Kirstin's mind to stop being my friend. It was impressive to me, mainly because I felt sure that I would not have been so easy on her were the tables turned. Had Kirstin started spending more time with a super-cool partying chick like Vera, I would have felt ditched, obsessed over what I had done wrong to be so alienated, and happily given her the cold shoulder when she came running back. Kirstin, on the other hand, had made great friends with other people in my absence, pursued her coursework, and generally didn't seem to notice at all that I had briefly left her orbit. I felt like an idiot.

And, though I felt a renewed affection for Kirstin (to this day, I consider her among the most wonderful people I've ever met) and tried not to let her out of my sights for very long the rest of that year, she still didn't have the one prevailing interest I required. Vera may have been out, but booze was still very much in. And so I grasped at the shirtsleeves of other big drinkers—*Hey! Take me with you!*—while I tried to find someone who drank as much as I did and whose company I actually enjoyed. I met nice enough people—hippies, misfits, arch party girls, and slackers—but I never felt connected to them and knew deep in my bones that, if they weren't partiers, we wouldn't be hanging out. I just desperately wanted company while I drank to oblivion and passed out. Most people I hung out with deserved a better friend than me. Though I already knew the terrible satisfaction of drinking alone, some part of me still craved that human connection. Already living life underwater, I grabbed at other people's legs as they swam by and tried to pull them down with me.

Until the twin miracles of sobriety and Facebook, I had never kept in touch with anyone very well, if at all. Dozens of friends and people I rather liked at one point have easily drifted from my view to gather dust in my memory. For years, I buried the thought of Vera and pined for the friendship of Kirstin. And, for as many years, I have regretted the many relationships I lost to my staggering inability to return phone calls or letters, rued the carelessness with which I treated friendships, and have been crushed by the guilt and embarrassment of feeling it is too late to try now.

When I finally got sober, I had spent so much time consumed with relationships that were based on drinking, I hadn't bothered to nurture any that weren't. I couldn't stand to be around drinking my first year clean, but had no one but drinkers to turn to. While alcohol gave me instant intimacy, which can be as dangerous as it can be seductive, making friends without booze was clumsy and sometimes embarrassing. It felt like dating without the electric thrill of romance and rife with awkward silences. Also, I didn't speak the language:

Normal Person: Do you want to go to dinner with us tonight?

Me: Oh, sorry, I don't drink anymore.

Normal Person: Um, okay. But do you want to come to dinner? We're going to Luna Café.

Me: What kind of twisted games do you people play out here in the so-called real world? Why on earth would anyone go to dinner and not get wasted? What, are you trying to get me to relapse, you sick fuck?!

On another occasion, after having tea with a woman I had just recently met and instantly dug, I said, "You know, I really like you. And that is saying something. I have a hard time connecting with people. God, that sounds so antisocial. I swear I'm not a sociopath!" And then I laughed nervously while she walked out of my apartment.

I soon realized that the people I considered my best friends had their own best friends and inner circles that didn't include me. Years of drinking and living only for fun had led to all those unreturned phone calls and e-mails, relationships that went untended, and the loss of friendships I thought would be forever. What had I done? Could I make new friends? I started by hovering over my colleagues like they were precious gifts I had never noticed before and making lists of the wives of Peter's friends I liked the most. I was annoying the crap out of everyone and getting nowhere. Until, that is, I had dinner with my old friend and co-worker Sophie.

"Sacha, omigod, I am so impressed and excited you are sober!" Sophie cried. "Do you know what? I am loving Pellegrino right now!" And we talked—really talked—for hours. She had left the media world and become a leader in the international human rights movement; she spoke Chinese; she was dating a kinda, sorta famous filmmaker; she still had dinner with her parents every week; and she still talked as though she'd seen behind the curtain of life and been awed and inspired—and maybe she has.

Recently, Sophie had a truly serious health emergency that required surgery, and she pondered her own death.

"I'm really lucky though, you know?" she said to me in my kitchen as she washed kale for dinner. "I'm two years older than my friend Carter was when he died of leukemia. I mean, I bet he'd have been happy with an extra two years."

It's a lot harder to make friends sober. You're pickier because you're not drinking through their flaws; but you're softer, too, because you see how deeply and profoundly flawed you are yourself. As I chain-smoked and drank away my twenties in a haze of denial and cynicism, I could have never truly *heard* Sophie when I was drinking. To feel lucky to have lived thirty-four years when a wonderful friend only made it to thirty-two is the kind of vision and insight that scared the shit out of me when I first met Sophie and was ingesting all kinds of poison every night. Now, I just want to be more like her. It turns out that I didn't need to make new friends after all. I just needed to take a closer look at all of the wonderful friends, like Kirstin and Sophie, I already had.

Number 5 on the Sacha Fantasy Relapse Pass: Parallel Universe

The theory of parallel universes says that every possible possibility is a real reality on some other plane of existence. Also known as the multiverse or many-worlds theory, the idea is that there are no absolutes in quantum mechanics; every predictable outcome corresponds to an alternate universe. Imagine throwing dice across a craps table. Maybe you're laughing, sipping champagne, and watching the little cubes float over the green felt on the table. The dice land. But the dice land thirty-six different times in thirty-six different combinations (from snake eyes to double sixes) in thirty-six different universes. But how predictable are you? Are you laughing in all thirty-six universes? That might depend on which combinations the dice have been landing. And, in turn, you might be throwing back a shot of whiskey, rather than clinking champagne glasses. As the possibilities are endless, so, too, are the universes.

And, somewhere out there, in some faraway universe, I am not an alcoholic. My fantasy, then, is to download my consciousness from this universe into the body of the nonalcoholic me living in another universe:

I wake up next to Peter in a hotel room in what I think is Tokyo. Our bed is perched next to a series of dramatic windows overlooking the city.

"Good morning," says Peter. "I'm omniscient. Welcome to the Thirty Nonillion, Eight Hundred Sextillion, and Three Universe!"

"I'm sorry, did you just say you were—"

"Omniscient, yes. Welcome!" says Peter. "What would you like to know about this universe? I can tell you anything. Would you like to know about quasars, local real estate, or beetles, for example? Or maybe the secrets of the universe, the question of life, the alpha and the omega—"

"I get it," I say, rolling my eyes. "You literally know it all."

"Did I mention you can drink as much as you like without guilt, fear, or consequence in this universe?" asks Peter gently.

"Why are we still talking?" I respond as I take in the

surroundings. Our room is vast. Overhead, there is a sky-light. The floor is a rich, dark wood. Sliding glass doors lead to a terrace with an infinity plunge pool and a Zen garden. To my left, a rice-paper wall slides open to reveal a room dotted with pillows—some large, some small, in silks, cottons, lamb's wool. I've always wanted a pillow room, I think to myself.

"Peter," I ask, "how did we get so rich?"

"Well," he begins with a warm smile, "first, your books sold so well, and then you did that supermodeling stint. Shall we toast to your success with a mimosa?"

As Omniscient Peter pops open the bottle of cham-pagne, he explains that I have become an important writer in this universe. Apparently, having spent my life sober, I have been prolific.

"Is that an Emmy?" I ask, pointing at a statuette in the corner and sipping my mimosa.

"Oh, yes!" exclaims Peter. "We just flew in from Hol-lywood. You won that for your work on the new HBO series—"

"Can I have another mimosa?" I ask. "And what's this about supermodeling? I seem to look the same."

"You are the same," says Peter. "We value the short in this universe."

We drink mimosas and laugh. We take in the city, stopping for cold chardonnay as we amble along a river. We drink scotch while we wait to be seated at a moody

Unwasted

candlelit restaurant. We drink velvet red wine and eat steak. We nurse glasses of cold vodka back in the infinity pool. I am never drunk, never guilty, never fearful. I find the urge to write is almost impossible to ignore. I don't feel denied anything; I have no discernible resentments. My biochemistry is magic. Still, I feel the tug of sadness pulling at my brain.

"Is this universe really real?" I ask Omniscient Peter.

"No, sweetheart," he whispers, pulling me close. "No, it's not real here. All fiction is its own universe. You wrote this world."

I decide to savor another drink before I have to leave.

Chapter 6

Monsoon wedding

Justin was actually much better looking than Jimmy Fallon, who was at the time my favorite *Saturday Night Live* player. And yet, as the vodka sloshed behind my eyes, I kept seeing Jimmy Fallon every time Justin turned toward me. Sometimes I would rub my eyes, shake my head, loosen up, roll my shoulders, and then look straight at Justin. And, for a moment, there he would be: officially very cute; no need to impose Jimmy Fallon over him. But, within seconds, it would happen again; the veil would descend and I would find myself talking to Jimmy Fallon. Looking back on it now, I think my subconscious was trying to tell me something about Justin's charms, not his appearance. I was beer-goggling his personality.

My close friend Ivy had organized a girls' weekend to Las Vegas, where I met Justin. Ivy grew up in the kind of

close-knit Chicago family who makes a trip to Vegas several
times a year—the way my family might go antiquing. Ivy's
Chicago friends and relatives were everything mine were not:
dozens of loud, silly, jubilant people—possibly all with serious gambling issues—who have huge Friday Night Dinners
("FNDs"), game nights, cooking competitions (the "Chicken
Parm Off" was particularly exciting), and three times the
number of nicknames as people in the room. They also are
always having so much fun, it never seems to occur to anyone to get seriously drunk or even to drink at all. I adore
each and every one of them. And especially Ivy, who makes
me feel home, safe, and loved every time I talk to her. Ivy
is also the only person I know incapable of schadenfreude
(which makes it particularly odd that we are so close) and
is an utterly engrossing conversationalist. She can knock me
out with a single question: "Do you think mutual respect or
shared values is more important in a relationship?" she once
asked in her casual and yet deeply interested way. Before sobriety, I would marvel at her fascination with moral questions and reach for the wispy threads of integrity dangling
out of reach in my mind. Things like "values" and "respect"
were not yet even on my list of relationship musts, which at
that point really only included "intimidatingly smart" and
"hysterically funny." I liked in particular to scoff at men who
thought books were objects one could leave behind once one
left college and at those who thought Dane Cook was awesome. Which brings us to Justin.

Unwasted

Our friend Emily came with Ivy and me to Vegas and promptly looked up her old camp pal, Justin, to come and hang out. Justin was a native of Las Vegas and the marketing director for a French-immersion charter school in the area. It all sounded so normal.

"I didn't think people actually lived in Vegas," I said to Ivy and Emily. "You know, except for showgirls and magicians."

"It's like the fastest-growing city in America, Sach," said Ivy.

"I guess I never really believed that," I said, as though such statistics were matters of opinion, and I suddenly became unnerved by the kind of person who thinks it's normal to raise children in Las Vegas and send them to, say, French-immersion charter schools in the shadow of a city in which strip clubs, casinos, and Celine Dion pass for culture.

But Justin seemed like a perfectly well-adjusted, sun-drenched blond. And, after dinner with the girls and after several cocktails and bottles of wine, we met Justin at a bar and he even seemed "hysterically funny." He had, of course, also morphed into Jimmy Fallon at that point. And, though I never found him "intimidatingly smart," a night on the town with Jimmy Fallon, er, Justin, seemed like a very Las Vegas thing to do.

I remember a night club, the kind of cheesy straight club where the guys wear too much gel in their hair and the girls look a lot more like MTV spring-breakers than, well, I do or ever did. It was like disco dancing at a reality-show casting call. There were a lot of laser-light-show effects and Usher remixes. I remember saying, "Hell yes, Jimmy Fallon," when Justin asked me if I wanted to get out of there. I remember saying good-bye to my girlfriends. I was on the heels of a breakup and I thought that spending the night with someone who wouldn't ask me about that would be a lot better than hanging out with the good friends who would. *Run away, Sacha, run away.*

In the next scene—for my memory has elided segments of the evening and edited the night into a short film—we were at an Irish pub. Or, at least, what passes for such in Vegas. It was a brand-new-but-made-to-look-old pub with shiny brass rails along the bar and four-leaf clovers dotting the wood-paneled walls.

"I thought this might be more your scene," said Justin, carrying two of the largest steins of beer I have ever encountered.

I'm not sure what about me screamed, "Fake authentic Irish pub, please," but, when the actually-from-Ireland Irish band started up nice and loud, complete with total audience participation, I at least didn't have to worry about keeping up a conversation. This was never more of a relief than when, during the band's break, Justin said, "That's what I love about Vegas. You don't have to travel because every place you'd want to go is already right here."

"Shhhh, Jimmy Fallon," I said, hand reaching up to

silence him. *Drink more, Sacha. Drink more.* Though, when the band covered the Violent Femmes in full Irish brogue, I was legitimately delighted with the choice of bar and began belting out "Blister in the Sun" with the regulars (or were they just handpicked codgers meant to look like genuine regulars in an Irish bar so that people like me would feel like I was having an authentic experience? "Vegas is meta," I whispered).

But then we were in a new scene. There was a bar in the middle of one of those Las Vegas hallway malls. It was in the shape of a large white orb—like being inside a bubble or maybe a geodesic dome. The drinks were all brightly colored: red, purple, and blue martinis bobbed along against the white bubble walls. *Want more, want more.*

"It's like being in space, right?" Justin asked, eyes wide and smiling, thrilled to be introducing me to Judy Jetson's favorite bar.

"You're funny, Jimmy Fallon."

"Why do you keep calling me that?"

"Shhhh."

Scene change: Sunlight is streaming through the curtains across a very lived-in bedroom. Laundry is heaped here and there, a model airplane rests on a desk, there are small trophies on a bookshelf, and a poster of a Lamborghini tacked to the wall. This is not my hotel room. *How the fuck did I get into a ten-year-old boy's room?* Suddenly, I am all too aware that the sunlight is new, that it is early,

like 7-A.M.-and-I-went-to-bed-at-4-A.M. early, but I have the
energy of the displaced, the vigor of the shamed. I simply
want nothing more than to teleport back to my own hotel bed
and wake up in the afternoon as though this never happened.
Like a normal person.

"Good morning," says a chipper voice in the doorway.
Justin. *Okay, no big deal. Justin is Emily's friend. He's a
nice, cute guy. Not the worst outcome.* Justin leans in the
doorway shirtless but wearing cargo shorts and sneakers as
though he has just spent the last hour mowing the lawn.

"Hi," I rasp, sounding a lot more like Stevie Nicks than I
had anticipated. "Where are we?"

"My house!"

"Your house?"

"Well, my parents' house. But don't worry, they're on vacation."

And, until that moment, I had not been worried at all
that his parents might actually be proximate because why
on earth would they be? Why would you take a girl to your
parents' house? When it occurs to me—

"Um, Justin, do you live with your parents?"

"I'm saving a lot of money, dude."

A peek out the window confirms that I am in the midst of
a labyrinth of suburban tract homes. There is nary a tree in
sight, and endless replicas of the same sandy-hued house and
two-car garage unfold into the distance over and over again.
Ivy was right about Vegas's fast growth; this sea of expansion

looks like it fell off the back of a flatbed truck pre-assembled in the middle of the night.

"Why are you up so early?" I ask in another Stevie Nicksian barfly rasp, feeling more and more out of place in the arrested development of Justin's childhood—and, apparently, adulthood—bedroom.

"I promised my parents I'd clean the pool before they came back," says Justin.

I decide not to question why he felt the crack of dawn was the right time to do this chore. But, if it's an invitation to go swimming, I'm passing. I am just grateful he is alert and can take me back to the city, to a room that does not make me feel like a child molester.

Justin enters the room and turns his back to me to open the door to his closet. And there, splashed across the entirety of his back, is the most insane and mortifying thing I have ever seen. It is a tattoo. But it is not a massive dragon or a red heart that says "Mom" or a Chinese character or any of the thousands of inane but entirely expected tattoos one might imagine. The tattoo is a cartoon man, a kind of stick figure Rastafarian (there are definitely dreadlocks emerging from its circle head), who is half-dancing and half-drinking a cup of coffee, arms akimbo, a mug in one hand. It is a happy Jamaican coffee drinker. It is a cartoon, but it also has the simplicity of a logo. The phrase "Jammin' Java Joe" ricochets in my head for a second, but then disappears. And I just gape at what has to be the least badass, most ridiculous, and possibly even racist tattoo that has ever seen the light of day. What self-respecting tattoo artist would even agree to render this embarrassment on a man's back?

"Awesome, right?" asks Justin, looking over his shoulder and noticing my jaw has unhinged itself from my body and landed on the floor. And I am embarrassed—not for me, but for Justin. *No, sweet, simple Justin. No. Bad idea. Baaad.* And then, as if saving the worst for last, Justin finds the T-shirt he has apparently been rooting around in the closet for. He pulls it over his head; the T-shirt is threadbare, light yellow, and, in small letters across the chest, reads: JAMMIN' JAVA JOE, MON. KINGSTON, JAMAICA. And I am already thinking, *No, no, no,* as he turns around to reveal a very colorful and large image of, well, Jammin' Java Joe on the back of the shirt. And as the fabric slides down Justin's back, the cartoon on the T-shirt neatly falls into place in perfect scale over the tattoo on Justin's body. Like lining up a tracing-paper illustration. An exact copy. Just like all the houses on his block.

And I realize: I did not hang out with Jimmy Fallon last night. I spent the night with Jammin' Java Joe. And that is when I am embarrassed for myself.

Back at the hotel, Ivy and Emily (and our friends Meri and Jodi) scream with laughter when I tell them about Jammin' Java Joe, when I tell them about Jimmy Fallon, and when I tell them about the Lamborghini poster. "I think I've even seen that T-shirt before," I say. "I think it's like a popular tourist shirt in Jamaica." And that is when Emily confesses

124

that Justin has been wearing that T-shirt since she met him at camp; that scrap of cloth must be at least fifteen years old. "He must be totally obsessed with it," she says. And we all fall across each other in tears laughing.

"I wish you had stayed around last night," Ivy says to me later. And I wish that as well. Why would I ditch a group of girls I have known since college and rarely see—none of whom live in the same city as I do—for Jammin' Java Joe? That's easy: Intimacy was precisely what I wanted to avoid that night. I didn't leave some of my best friends for some guy; I left my best friends for more mindless drinking—a lot more than I would have gotten away with if I'd stayed with them. I wanted more alcohol, more fun, more Vegas, more alcohol, more, more, more. And, so I took it. But I soon became aware of a strong sense of guilt creeping into my psyche, a familiar echo based on thousands of poor choices.

Entitlement was the insidious little thread that snaked through my alcoholism. I wanted what I wanted when I wanted it. And if what I wanted conflicted with your plans, I did it anyway. I would call when it was convenient for me, cancel plans when a better option came along, and I sure as shit would drink with Jimmy Fallon whenever I wanted.

A couple of years after that trip and brimming with one too many drunken regrets, I got sober and thought maybe now I would stop feeling so guilty and panicky all the time. It turns out, though, that ditching the booze removes a symptom of the narcissistic alcoholic, but it doesn't cure you. Sure,

I felt better in the mornings, made fewer impulsive late-night decisions, and stopped confusing people for the cast of *Saturday Night Live*, but I unconsciously started to look for new ways to fill the void alcohol left in its wake, the void left by alcohol's warm embrace and internal whisper: *Go ahead, have fun. Fuck it. Drink more, play more. You're entitled.*

There were far more hours in the day than I had ever realized. When you aren't hung-over or just plain exhausted from the night before, the week before, the month before, time slows way, way down and practically asks, "Well, are you going to do something with your sobriety, doll, or should I just fast-forward to your death?" I began to drift in and out of fugue-like states; weeks would pass and I wouldn't notice it, couldn't tell you what I had been up to at work, and didn't know what day it was. I may not have been hung over, but I sure was bored.

You know what I needed—no, *deserved?* Whatever the hell I wanted. I had quit drinking, damn it. Where was my prize? So I got my hair done at the fancy place. I got a facial; I paid ahead for a series of facials. I bought a really good winter coat, leather boots, and a cashmere scarf and hat set. I'd be glad I did that when winter rolled around. Plus, I *needed* nice clothes for my new job. Maybe all new clothes. I'd go to the Bluefly website, select every outfit I wanted from the entire site, click it into my shopping bag, and then mull over my choices at the end. When I couldn't decide what to throw back to the Internet and what to pay for, I'd just buy it all.

Fuck it. I also threw myself into my garden, which suddenly I thought really should have a few dozen more pots and flowers. And a good bench—with all-weather cushions from Restoration Hardware. A thousand dollars for the garden was really a quality-of-life issue anyway.

Instead of drinking, I ignored my credit limits, ignored my status as an adult, and I spent. And spent and spent. I was an Internet shopper, combing through sites looking for everything from new books to yoga duds (because, even if I didn't practice yoga right now, I might if I had the right gear). I would literally brainstorm personal flaws and look for products to solve them: I'd Google everything from "longer eyelashes" to "more energy" and see what the Internet would bring back to me—and then I'd buy it. Instead of actually becoming the person I wanted to be, I just looked the part.

But worse than the out-of-control spending were the lies. I calmly told Peter I had no credit-card debt while I juggled my balances between various low-APR offers in a kind of personal-finance Three-card Monte that kept me up nights and returned me to the panicked states I had given up drinking to relieve myself of in the first place. Back when Ivy's sad eyes told me she wished I hadn't run off with Justin, I shuddered. Now, every time Peter went to get the mail, I shuddered.

Why did I always feel entitled to fill the void with something that was bad for me? I never turned to, say, writing as a way to sate the hole inside. *There's no more alcohol? Oh,*

I know, I'll just write that novel I've always been planning. I'll just spend eight hours at a stretch creating a master-piece. Or: I can't have alcohol? Maybe I should just spend my days doing more aerobic exercise. I'll just pop in an ultimate-fitness video and hit REPEAT *until I look like Dara Torres.* No, such pursuits wouldn't work at all. Apparently, the void inside me must be filled with something that makes me feel awful about myself. It wouldn't do to replace my alcoholism with a successful career and more cardio. *How's sobriety? Well, it's just great. I wrote a critically acclaimed novel as well as a lucrative best-seller, and my ass looks fantastic!* Which, honestly, begs the question: Why on earth do I have a void in my soul that can only be filled by some-thing masochistic? It's a disturbing reality to come to terms with. Some sick part of me needs to hurt myself in order to feel whole, comfortable in my skin, and just plain all right. So my challenge is either to fill the void with something that does not invite misery or else to make peace with the void.

By the time I had $30,000 of debt, I couldn't even re-member what I had spent it on or what I had to show for it. I just knew I needed to pay it all back before Peter found out. Because if he knew how sick and crazy I really was, he'd leave me in a heartbeat. And that would be it for me. Forget sobriety, forget work, forget life, losing Peter would be an unsurvivable hurt.

When I met Peter, while we were both working at *The New Republic*, he read something I wrote, pulled me aside,

128

and said, "We've got to get you writing more." At a magazine where I had consistently told myself I didn't belong, where I had countless times reminded myself that I was a fluke hire, and assured myself that the vast majority of writers there did not respect me, Peter saw and often said something else: "You've got something"; "I just found my favorite columnist"; "Shut up and write." And I watched him comb the hallways, teasing the interns, pulling a writer into his office, sitting down with the fact-checkers for come-to-Jesus meetings about his concerns, his baritone caroming along the narrow halls. I memorized his footfalls and knew when he approached. I gobbled up his arguments, his wit, even his exasperations.

I thought about Ivy's question: "Do you think mutual respect or shared values is more important in a relationship?" I didn't think Peter and I shared values. Peter regretted never joining the Marines. I regretted never going to Mardi Gras pre-Hurricane Katrina. But respect. Now that was where things became interesting. It wasn't just that Peter respected me; it was that someone I so deeply respected in return respected me. I had precious few friends I could say this about (primarily because I cynically respected so few people to begin with) and even fewer friends who championed me so enthusiastically. Ivy was one. She makes me feel like everything I do, I should do more of; she inspires me. And all the while this poker-obsessed school principal from Chicago lives with a grace and integrity (her love of family, her devotion to her best friends, her philosophical poignancy) that I used to find unusual, even quaint.

Peter has never found values to be either unusual or quaint. And, by the time I realized I had none, I was gob-smacked in love. Getting sober was in part an effort to sever myself from a deep loneliness, a sense that no one really understood me. Because, whether it was Peter or someone else, no quality man or friend worth his salt, no person of any integrity or excellence, was going to stick around for me very long while I was drinking. And I didn't want to end up surrounding myself with people I needed to be wasted around just to tolerate. I didn't want to ditch my friends for Jammin' Java Joe anymore.

I just wish I had realized then that abandoning drinking would not, in and of itself, magically turn me into a person of values. The panic I felt from replacing alcohol with a far less satisfying shopping spree was due to a fear of getting caught—not from a fear of lying, which like any good alcoholic I did almost as much as blinking ("Seriously, I only had two drinks"; "It was really, really cheap, I swear"). I didn't feel like a liar, though; I just felt like Peter and I weren't on the same page about spending or about how much things should cost—or how much I was entitled to. Just like I used to feel like no one understood that I needed more wine than most people; and just like I used to feel like Peter and I weren't on the same page about drinking. As though being on different pages was not a lie or a lack of shared values; as though being on different pages was simply a hiccup between us that I would hide by secretly drinking or by secretly spending. At the time, had you asked me if I was I liar, I would have honestly said no.

I thought I filled the void inside me with alcohol and then shopping because no one understood me, because no one knew the real me, because no one got that I needed more and more and more and more. I had more of a thirst than most people. I was just special that way. But that was the biggest lie I told—and I told it to myself. I didn't *need* more of anything; I just *wanted* more. And plenty of people were quite capable of understanding that, of seeing the real me; they just weren't going to stick around for it. You don't get to spend your way into massive debt and still have a partner who says, "No problem." You don't get to shroud every interaction with your partner in alcohol and then pretend you have an authentic relationship.

And so, for me, it was not the moment of putting down the drink that eliminated my entitlement to more and more and more; it was putting down the credit cards that did it. Just like with drinking, the funny thing about debt is that it doesn't budge until you're honest about it. After all, I had to maintain the appearance of someone who didn't have debt around Peter, which meant I was saying yes to all kinds of little expenses I ought not to have. And then Peter tried to re-finance our apartment. And guess whose credit wasn't, heh, stellar anymore? Whoops!

Sacha Z. Scoblic

Trying to hide from the person you live with is extremely difficult; trying to hide from the person you like and love most in the world is pure hell. Once Peter's rage over the debacle of my debt subsided, I was left with his disappointment. It had never occurred to Peter before that moment that I was even *capable* of deceiving him so spectacularly. Oddly, it had never occurred to me, either.

Though I instinctively hate aphorisms, here's one I do like: "You're only as sick as your secrets."

I told Amy everything about my fiscal inebriation, my emotional sobriety relapse. And I began attending twelve-step meetings with far more regularity than I had been—because I have found that every day I go to a meeting is a day I don't drink and also a day I don't lie. There's just something about spending time with a bunch of crazy alcoholics trying to do their best in this life that helps me walk the line. Honesty is now the salve I apply to the void when I hear it whisper in a dark voice, "He just doesn't understand that you need more." Because the faster I am honest, the faster the problem goes away.

Recently, I bounced a check. It was an ordinary miscalculation—an honest, good old-fashioned mistake. But when Peter discovered it—because Peter, heh heh, opens all the mail in our house now—my mind immediately reverted to scrambling for an excuse, an out, a lie. I could feel lies racing across my brain—*it's obviously a bank mistake; I already took care of that online; the post office sent the check too*

132

slowly—and I felt panic creep into my chest while my face clenched defensively. And then I remembered: I'm not hiding anything. I didn't bounce a check because I bought new shoes or because I drank too much. I didn't have to lie. Relief flooded my system as I said, "Yikes. I better take care of that." Nothing quite helps me achieve serenity more than the knowledge that I have done nothing wrong that day, that I have lied to no one, that I have nothing to feel guilt or panic over.

Nowadays, I just tell the truth and brace myself for what I often assume is the inevitable storm: "I can't make it to your dinner party, because I am exhausted and just want to stay home and watch a movie"; "I did hear you ask me to do that, boss, and I'm sorry I dropped the ball"; "I'm an asshole, and I forgot to feed your cat all weekend while you were away." But usually there's no storm to brace against; usually people instantly recognize and respect the truth. Even my friends Noam and Amy—though they have understandably never asked me to cat-sit again.

And honesty means something else, too. When I am honest about who I want to be surrounded by—Ivy instead of Jammin' Java Joe, for instance—I can have a very good time sober. I think often of Ivy's family, laughing so hard no one even thinks to ask for a drink. I remember all of the times someone asked me if I could have a good time without drinking and I couldn't understand what the point of even trying such a thing would be. And now I know. Now, when Peter and

I make our own Friday Night Dinner and I can feel the sweet anticipation of the weekend rushing toward me, when Peter looks for good movies or yells at the TV upon finding none, when our dog, SciFi, reaches up my legs looking for just a bite of whatever I'm making ("I can have some?"), when I relate some silly story from the week and Peter cracks up, when Peter kisses my forehead and says, "I've never loved you more," when I bask in knowing that I get to share my life with this man, when every evening with him is a party, when every night is ours—that is when I know why I am sober. Because I remember all of it. Because none of it is relegated to a blackout, because none of it led to drunken drama, because at no point did I feel like I needed more. When you finally realize how much you have, it's pretty hard to feel entitled to more.

The day Peter and I got married, it rained. Biblically. Torrents and sheets of water hurled themselves at the streets, pelting pedestrians mercilessly as I watched, my face pressed against the glass of a beauty salon window. At three o'clock in the afternoon on a summer day, the sky turned its deepest black and oceans of precipitation flooded the streets of Washington while lightning coursed maniacally through the air. *They're never going to let us on the roof of the Hay-Adams,* I thought. The hotel that was a past setting of a drunken mishap would now be the launch point for a new life. I thought about how I wasn't entitled to a sunny day, that I should lose my attachment to what I wanted and embrace what I had. I turned from the window as my mother, Peter's mother, and a gaggle of hairdressers and salon staff stood quietly and looked at me with a barely contained concern.

"Well, it's gonna be a long, happy marriage!" I cheered, as the assembled crowd breathed a collective sigh of relief that the bride was not about to lose it.

And I called Peter then to laugh about the crazy rain. I was about to marry Peter. Peter, whom I could talk to until the wee hours of the morning and it would never grow dull. Peter, who thinks books make a home. Peter, whose arms create a safe place to fall, whose breath gives me light. Peter, who loves a good thunderstorm as much as I do. Why on earth would a little rain bother me? This was the best day of my life. "I love you so much," I said, as I watched the monsoon gathering strength outside the salon window.

We met our photographer at 5 o'clock that evening in the Hay-Adams for a few pictures before the 6 o'clock ceremony—still tentatively planned for the rooftop. Peter and I posed and smiled awkwardly in our wedding costumes, when the photographer suddenly looked up from behind the camera and pointed to the window. Sunlight was streaming in. The three of us ran through the hotel and then outside as steam lifted off the sidewalks and the smell of ozone coated the air. I held up my dress and we skipped across the street and into Lafayette Square Park—an enchanted wonderland of dew drops and glittery sunlight and mist. By the time we said our vows, a strong evening sun had dried the day and warmed the rooftop.

A surprising thing happened when I stopped feeling entitled to things: I gained more than I ever knew I wanted. Because, finally, for the first time—and gratefully—all that I have, I came by honestly.

Number 6 on the Sacha Fantasy Relapse Pass: Let's Put the "Fantasy" into "Fantasy Relapse"

Heretofore, life had been simple for the young maiden called Sacha. The daughter of the village wizard, education was valued in her cottage home, and she had been encouraged to study archery, runes, and alchemy. She was named Sacha after the goddess of insight and visions—Psyacha—and indeed had proved to be a quick-witted and intuitive girl. She seemed to know when a villager was about to die, could predict the weather, and had uncanny powers of persuasion. Once, when Sacha was but a child of three celestial years, she had eluded the grasp of the evil and powerful Lord Gorgon. Gorgon had kidnapped Sacha in the hope of grooming the small child to become his chief oracle. But Sacha escaped by convincing the drunken trolls who had been left to guard her that she wasn't actually real. Sacha returned to her village unscathed, but the swooning and gullible trolls had made an impression—and Sacha swore she would never sip from a potion, tonic, or elixir of any substantial potency.

Many would-be suitors in the village wooed Sacha, but the young maiden could not help but think that she was meant for something greater than the pedestrian affairs of the heart. And so it was that the fair Sacha had grown up to be a young lady with lips that had touched neither wine nor men. But the hands of fate were about to change all of that.

One day, as Sacha was riding her unicorn, Zephyr, through the forest, she came upon three elves.

"Milady," said one, "we are the Elves of the Golden Orb. We seek the one in this region who is called Sacha."

"I am Sacha," said Sacha, for she was.

"And we are Mozer, Banxie, and Pip," said Pip, the eldest elf, whose beard nearly touched the curled toes on his buckled leather booties. He explained to Sacha that the Elves of the Golden Orb had protected daylight from Lord Gorgon for thousands of years.

"If it were up to Lord Gorgon," said Pip, "the demi-world would fall into a permanent bacchanalian nighttime in which the troll would lie with the unicorn, the minstrels would play intense metallic chords, and all the creatures of the demi-world would revel and undulate at the feet of Gorgon himself."

Mozer and Banxie quivered, their eyes large and misty as Pip spoke.

"How awful!" cried Sacha, who had always secretly thought that the demi-world already had too much night-time, thank you very much.

"And now he is close to achieving his goal," continued Pip. "Lord Gorgon has perfected a new spell that will scare the sun away, leaving the demi-world to nothing but the light of the moon. But, according to the ancient scrolls, the spell will only work at midnight on this very night."

"How can we stop this fiendish plot?" asked Sacha.

"We need you, Sacha, Daughter of the Wizard, to use your magical powers of persuasion on Gorgon," said Pip. "Talk the dark lord out of his evil plan!"

Mozer and Banxie fell to their knees chanting, "Please, please, please."

Sacha briefly considered riding Zephyr back to her village to warn her parents, but before she even saw the smoke rising over the trees, Sacha psychically knew her family had been killed.

"He's looking for me," she whispered to herself. Then she faced the Elves of the Golden Orb and declared, "I'll do it! But put on your capes; it's about to rain."

The quartet hiked for hours—up craggy peaks, down bottomless ravines, and through enchanted forests, where they battled wood gnomes and black spirits before the fickle forest fairies would let them pass. On the way, Banxie had been shot with an arrow and Mozer had eaten poison berries, but Pip healed both with ancient elfin medicines, and the group forged onward. It was nearly half past eleven by the time they reached Lord Gorgon's castle.

Darkness had fallen across the lands of the demi-world and eerie mists rose from the shadows. Thunder menaced the skies and strange green lights emanated from Gorgon's inner sanctum.

"Lady Sacha," said Pip, "before we go in, you must drink this special elixir I have prepared. It is very potent. It will give your words even more power than they already have."

Mozer and Banxie exchanged a concerned look.

"But I do not partake of elixir," said Sacha.

"The fate of the demi-world rests in your hands," said Pip as he handed her the amber fluid.

As Sacha drank, she noticed Mozer and Banxie huddled together, whispering frantically to one another.

"Uh, Pip?" said Mozer. "I don't think she was supposed to drink the elixir."

"I'm not even sure the elixir is meant for, you know, this particular end-of-the-demi-world scenario," added Banxie.

"That's funny," replied Pip, "because it really didn't feel right. Even as I was giving it to her, I think I knew something was off."

"Shtupid elfs," hiccupped Sacha.

An hour later, Sacha was dancing to the metallic chords of the minstrels in Lord Gorgon's tower.

"Glow stick?" Gorgon asked, passing her an electric green tube.

"Don't mind if I do," she giggled. The pair kissed, and then Sacha asked, "Would you like something more to drink, my lord?"

"Always," replied Gorgon.

"Mozer! Banxie!" screamed Sacha. "Fetch Lord Gorgon and me some more elixir. And tell Pip to put extra magic mushrooms in it this time or I'll feed him to the dragon."

"Yes, Lady Sacha," the two elves chanted in unison as they walked around Zephyr and a troll nuzzling and shuffled off into the permanent nighttime.

"I just love a good bacchanalia, don't you?" said Gorgon to no one in particular as he flashed a wicked smile and all the creatures of the demi-world undulated at his feet.

Chapter 7
Choosing My Religion

"**P**ray," said Amy as she tried on a fuchsia hat the size of a satellite dish and appraised herself in the mirror. When you drive a convertible Porsche and have a buzz cut, as Amy does, hats apparently play a major role in your life. "Ask God for strength."

"Oh, Jesus Christ," I replied.

"That's a start," she teased, tossing the hat aside. "I can get that hat cheaper at Eastern Market."

I'd just let Amy in on the fact that I wasn't exactly kosher with the whole God thing. Every twelve-step meeting was riddled with God and higher powers. Which was great—for other people. Wasn't there a Universalist meeting or something, maybe a Po-Mo rap session? There must be a way to have a spiritual sobriety without a higher power. Hell, the Buddhists have been at it for thousands of years.

Sacha Z. Scoblic

I grew up without religion. My family is composed of a mishmash of Judeo-Christian traditions, and I was brought up without a particular allegiance to any one strain. On the few occasions I did enter a house of worship—after sleeping over at a friend's, for a Bar mitzvah, or when my mom dragged me to midnight mass on Christmas—I never really got it. All of the Biblical "characters," with their strange languages, sins, and old-fashioned hymns, struck me as a little creepy. And because most religious people I met seemed to be about my grandparents' age, I thought that perhaps religion itself was an anachronism, fading from modern favor. (Imagine my surprise when I went to college and met all kinds of young, fervent big-church Christians ready to fight for my soul and young, activist Jews who wanted me to fight for a homeland.) Needless to say, growing up, I never thought too deeply about any of this stuff. Listening to people in the rooms of a twelve-step meeting invoke God as though we all shared the same beliefs continually hit my ears wrong. I wanted to stop drinking, not get a new religion.

Of course, my own ideas about spiritual life had heretofore led me to believe that a weekend alone with a lot of booze, cigarettes, and cable television was heaven. So perhaps I wasn't the greatest arbiter of spiritual depth. Besides, maybe if I became a more soulful person, I would also become a more likeable person. As it was, I had a small eye-rolling and people-hating problem. And I had to admit, I *felt* spiritually bereft. Religious talk may have turned me off, but I recognized that I did not have a cogent set of principles and beliefs to live by.

I know religion fills the alcoholic void for a lot of people, like the millions who find solace from addiction not in any twelve-step program but in the church. For many, filling the addiction inside and assuaging the void left behind by the toxins means finding God—putting a whole new spin on religion as an opiate for the masses. Even outside of any church, I have heard people refer to a "God-shaped hole." I'd like to smack those people. Except that the idea seems to work for some nice folks, and who am I to darken the doorways of their happiness?

The problem with bumper-sticker aphorisms is that they lack nuance. And it is in the nuance where you find all the really sweet, juicy nuggets in life. And the entire idea of a God-shaped anything takes for granted a lot of things I think should not be—like, for instance, God. And, out of all ideas, certainly the idea of God is a shade of gray. Plus, the whole phrase makes me think of distracting literalities like shapes: Is God trapezoidal? Also, a "God-shaped hole inside" just ends up sounding like a dirty euphemism. Though, I suppose, if my hole inside were in fact God-shaped, the smart thing to do would be to simply fill it up by believing in God. Kind of like playing the odds or buying in to Pascal's Wager: If there's no God, what's the harm in believing, and, if there is a God, won't I be relieved that I paid lip-service to him when the Rapture comes and the hole in my soul knits back

143

together? Perhaps. And perhaps attending to my spirit will indeed manifest the required sincerity for such an endeavor, and belief will follow action.

Hence, I turned my attention to mustering up a prayer. Amy said prayer would help me with my urge to drink. My stubbornness. My grumpiness. My overall, heh, mood. And so, one night, I curled in bed around Peter and seriously thought about saying a prayer. And that was as far as I got.

The problem was that prayer, to me, implied worship. And just what was I worshipping here? I didn't believe in God. How do you pray to something when you don't know what it is—or if it is? Well, if you're me, then you spend the better part of an all-nighter throwing recovery literature across the room, offering to reach down your throat and pull your heart out of your chest as a sacrifice for this so-called God, and then rock on your heels like a crazy person for a few hours while contemplating just how alone we all are floating out here in space by ourselves.

First, there was a ball of energy. The energy expanded rapidly and—*bang!*—the universe was created and continued to expand, and expand, and expand, as it still does today. And on at least one rock warmed by a star, the right gases and the raw materials for biology combined in such a way that life clambered out of the primordial ooze. Over the millennia, human beings with advanced intellect and consciousness emerged. But where did consciousness come from? And why did we humans crave a code for morality, an ethos of right and wrong? Dogs came out of the ooze, too, and they don't ponder guilt. Perhaps there was a God, a kind of infinite force that sculpted the conditions in which moral creatures could emerge. Then again.

Then again, perhaps out there in space beyond our current ken, there is another rock warmed by a star on which the right gases and the raw materials for biology combined in such a way that alien life rose from the murk. But maybe these gases and biota were just a bit different from those that formed Earth. Perhaps the brains of the aliens created on this rock are more highly developed than ours and their consciousness is collective and telepathic. Perhaps out there exists a race in which what is good for one is de facto good for all and vice versa; and a decision made by one is made by all. There is no crime nor punishment—just a cooperative of aliens, like a school of electric eels, working in tandem, with little use for the constraints of language or the tedium of the written word. This race just is. This race has no need for morality lessons, philosophy, passion plays, religion, or folklore.

If God can create the conditions for both moral and amoral creatures, then perhaps God isn't very concerned with right and wrong. In which case, he certainly doesn't care whether I drink or not. Perhaps God is a mad scientist in a world so vast and timeless our brains would melt should we somehow comprehend it all. Our entire infinite universe is contained in God's petri dish whilst he and his colleagues simply observe.

Or, worse, our entire universe is the flea circus God gives his kid to play with—and we are the fleas. We are simplistic, minute, and expendable.

Still, none of this—the amoral aliens, the flea circus, the mad scientist, the moral animals called Earthlings—none of this tells me where we are. If we are in some giant's snow globe, where did the giant come from and how did the giant's world begin? If our universe is the only universe, then where did that initial ball of energy that spurred the Big Bang originate? Who lit the match? Stephen Hawking thinks there's no need for God because our universe can in fact create something out of nothing; the universe can create a big old bang where once there was blankness. But why is there—or was there—blankness to begin with? If I keep going beyond the universe, beyond time, beyond the Big Bang, what kind of nothing is out there and where did it start?

"I am literally having a spiritual crisis," I told Peter when he found me at 3 A.M. hugging my knees in a corner of the living room. "We're so vulnerable just sitting on this planet waiting for the universe to inevitably contract and end us all."

Peter, who specializes in nuclear war with an abiding interest in climate change and all other existential threats to Earth, nodded. "Yep," he said. This was old news for my Czar of the Apocalyptic, my Secretary of Global Destruction, my Captain of Calamity. And, in a very sincere way, I understood Peter better. Why devote your life to, say, scribbling about books and culture and politics, as I do, when our entire species seems hell-bent on a suicidal arms race between human-made disaster, like nukes and global warming, and the already perilous course of things: The entire fucking planet is circling a dying star and, once the universe stops expanding, we'll all be crushed in a cosmic vacuum. That is, if the asteroids don't get us first.

"Fuck me," I said.

"Yep," Peter said again.

"The whole situation is just totally precarious."

"Yep."

I didn't exactly see God in any of this, let alone a spirit being I could talk to. I told Amy that I was having trouble praying to a "God"; she paused, finished applying her lipstick, narrowed her gaze, and simply said, "Do it anyway." Amy wasn't asking me to believe in anything; she was just asking me to behave as though I did. To act "as if." Which seemed a little weird to me. It was a gesture that reminded me of those people who say things like, "Dress for the job you want, not the job you have"—a philosophy that always struck me as overemphasizing appearance over substance. (*Maybe get the GED before the three-piece suit, you mail-room jackass.* Did I just think that?) But, as I was pretty much ready to stand on my head and speak in tongues if Amy asked me to (I found her simultaneously empathetic and always ready to kick the shit out of me), I decided to give it a shot. And so, with my best dress-for-success attitude, I looked to the ceiling the next night and decided to act *as if* I were a casual believer—as opposed to a zealot. Baby steps.

"Hi, H.P.," I said aloud to my bedroom, staring up at the ceiling (addressing my "higher power"—not Hewlett-Packard). "I am praying for serenity and the willingness to keep doing this. Um, thanks, dude."

Admittedly, it wasn't Shakespeare, nor my finest theatrical performance (my finest theatrical performance was circa 1990, when I spent an hour convincing my mother that the excruciating exhaust-pipe burn on my ankle was from a pizza oven at work and not from a motorcycle). But damn if I didn't feel a small sense of potency from getting quiet and saying words like *serenity* and *willingness* out loud. If my half-assed prayer gave me a tiny droplet of peace, imagine what a lifetime of prayer and hard-core meditation could yield me. I started to imagine a "spirit" room in my future mansion that would be dotted with Nepalese prayer flags, meditation pillows, miniature gongs, and guided imagery CDs by Deepak Chopra. I've no doubt there are excellent neurological explanations for why prayer brings peace to people; I don't believe talking to my ceiling actually connects me to a divine being. But then, why argue with results?

There is also, I am sure, a logical explanation as to why I have a vivid and inexplicable memory trapped in my brain from childhood that I can still see in my mind's eye as clearly as I can see my hands in front of me now. But I've tried not to argue too hard with this mystery; I simply like it too much. It

happened at age three, when my parents took me to a party—
the kind of party where eventually all the small children, as
I was, are put to sleep amongst the coats and purses that are
strewn across the guest bedroom duvet while the older kids
watch the adults mingle below from their perches at the top
of the banister. My family left very late; I vaguely recall my
father scooping me from the car in front of our house, his feet
crunching in the snow, and asking me if I was okay to walk.
We held hands and made our way up the shoveled path to
where my mother had stopped.

"Look at the moon, Sachie," my mother said. "Can you
see the man in the moon?"

My father kneeled down beside me to point up at the huge,
full, glowing moon planted directly over our house.

I can remember the profound sense of awe and magic I
felt in that moment, face turned skyward. How often do I
see the moon nowadays and not fully grasp the wild fact of
its orbit around us, its pull on our tides, its cosmic radiance?
Children see things with fresh eyes. Imagine seeing the moon
for the first time—a resplendent floating globe that follows
you wherever you look. Whether it was the first or the tenth
time I had truly faced the moon, it was a strange and en-
chanting moment. So, when my mother asked me if I saw
the man in the moon, I made a close inspection. And, though
surely my mom intended to point out the face she saw across
the full surface of the moon the way one might see an angel in the clouds (*See how those craters make the eyes and*

below there's a mouth?), I saw a man *on* the moon, not *in* the moon. I saw a small figure walking ever so slowly across the top of the moon itself—not peering out from within it. There, on top of the iridescent orb was an astronaut, with his bulky white space suit and round helmet. I had learned all about Neil Armstrong and walking on the moon. My vision seemed completely reasonable. Why wouldn't there be an astronaut on the moon? And why not tonight? The moon was so close in that frigid night, and I was positive my parents and I were all gazing upon the same lunar marvel, assured by the captivation reflected in their own gazes that they, too, could see my astronaut. So I waved. I waved at the man on the moon as my breath danced on the icy air. And my waving must have caught his attention.

Because he waved back.

It was almost as though he were made of the moon itself. He glowed in his white space suit as intensely as the celestial body on which he stood. He seemed to issue from it as he stood now, legs planted firmly at hip distance apart, and slowly waved at the small child far below who wondered how he kept from falling off.

And my parents were so delighted. I thought they were as tickled by this late-night meeting as I was. I thought that this must be a very rare and special encounter. Though now I can see that a tiny little girl, stuffed into her winter coat and waving at the moon like it was heaven above, is pretty delightful on its own without the need for a mass delusion.

Unwasted

I am a reasonable person. I know that, in order to see a man on the moon, the man would be nothing short of a giant taller than the Empire State Building. I know, too, that I myself would be invisible from space no matter how close in orbit the moon was that cycle. And, finally, I know the last manned mission to the moon happened a full year before I was born. And yet, there is that crisp, perfect, transcendent moment lodged in my brain along with all the other greats— the Peter files, the abiding love of Indian food, publishing my first article, my new kid sister throwing her arms around me.

Obviously, I was unintentionally cued by my parents into creating this luminous apparition and—the imagination of a child being as rich and unobstructed as any artist's—I created something so powerful and memorable, it seemed real. (I am quite sure that, though my family had just spent the evening at a party in the mid seventies, I had not ingested anything hallucinogenic.) I talked about the man on the moon for years. I wrote stories about him in school. I drew pictures of him in all of my notebooks. And, on dark nights, when there was a full moon, I would gaze out the window expectantly, hopefully. That I never saw him again only added to my strong sense that I had witnessed a once-in-a-lifetime event; I had been struck by lunar lightning.

Maybe that's why people say children are close to God— because children have such a visceral sense of awe. For years, the moon man intrigued me; for years, I believed sincerely that I had seen something precious and thrilling. My brain lit up in new ways when I pondered the moon man and, when I waited for his return under my bedroom window, I was wonder-filled. So, as I began to see the power in saying, "God, grant me the serenity," every time I had to face the boss who yelled, had to appear bright and shiny at a work cocktail reception, or had to take the heat for my own mistakes, it no longer seemed to matter if I actually believed in God or not. That there are logical explanations for the sense of calm that comes from saying calming words is something I find reassuring. I am a cynical adult who often forgets to notice the wonder around her; so learning the literal explanations for the effects of, say, prayer on the brain makes me more likely to do it. Knowing that prayer can release serotonin and oxytocin just gives me more incentive. Bring on the mood-altering chemicals! And, again, why argue with results? I have found moments of prayer, as I snuggle into my white bed in my deep blue bedroom—like a woman floating on her own moon—when I get grateful about the man next to me, my little pooch, my groovy neighborhood, and our good health and lives, in which I can rediscover a sense of adventure about life and I can touch a small and wonder-filled current inside of me. Because who the fuck would have guessed a few years ago that I would be this happy now?

When I drank, there were so many consequences. Happiness could scarcely make an appearance in a life spent shucking and jiving, lying and hiding, sleeping and zoning out. I was always late for work, loath to work, unmotivated,

and apt to watch twelve-hour marathons of television shows I
professed to hate. Sobriety didn't cure those traits, but it did
start to make me a lot more honest about them.

"Hey babe," I would say to Peter on the phone from the
office. "I'm surfing the Web and not doing anything I am
supposed to be doing and just feel like a total slag. Can you
kick my ass a little?"

"I tell you what," Peter would reply. "Do one hour of
really focused work right now—no excuses—and I'll call you
back to check in on your progress."

Sobriety was giving me a chance to unravel all of my
terrible instincts. And prayer gave me an opening to ap-
preciate the great fortune I did have in life, and, in turn, I
became more eager to protect that life, work for it, earn it,
do right by it. Prayer, despite my zero-tolerance policy for
burning-bush religious hallucinations, had turned out to be
a good tip. And it occurred to me that Amy and indeed other
twelve-steppers might have more good tips. It also occurred
to me that I was spectacularly awful at running my life. I
had, after all, once woken up at 10 A.M. on a workday to find
the table in my living room inexplicably overturned and with
what must have been several whole carrots' worth of carrot
shavings weaved throughout my hair like some kind of hag-
gard vitamin A mermaid with no memory at all of the night
before; undeterred, I got so wasted that very next night that
I had a seizure on the floor of a nightclub and was escorted
out only to find I had a crippling sense of sheer panic that I

couldn't shake for a week. I was so twitchy, I'd scream every time the phone rang and suffered through agonizing night terrors every time I closed my eyes. Maybe I shouldn't be the captain of this here ship. Why not try listening to what other people with more together lives had to say and follow their advice? Nowadays, I ask for advice a lot; whenever I am at a decision point, I run my problem by a few people and pay attention to their advice before acting. And, when I am in doubt or all alone, I try to get really, really quiet, focus, and listen carefully to my heart's desire. And then I do the precise opposite.

As I continued to be open to opinions other than my own, I began to see the power of community. A while back, for example, I didn't know how to handle a difficult colleague. Elizabeth had been giving me the cold shoulder for weeks—I mean a real old-fashioned Amish shunning. One day, things were fine; the next, I had leprosy. Now, Lord knows, I am a deeply flawed person, verbally impulsive, and no doubt capable of truly offending the hell out of someone. So I was quite certain that I had done something spectacularly awful. The problem was: I couldn't for the life of me think what it was. I scoured my recent memory for our interactions and came up empty. So I decided to buy Elizabeth a present. This is an odd instinct I occasionally have (*LOVE ME! It's a fucking present!*), one I am trying to eschew. Luckily, before I ran to the nearest store, I asked Peter, Amy, a colleague, and a few sober women for their input instead of relying on my wayward nature. (Once again, I should not be the captain of this here ship.) The results were fantastic: I ended a weeks-long office cold war over a perfectly civil lunch. Shocker: It was a simple miscommunication that was easily resolved. Relying on the group (who gave me refreshingly simple advice: "Be honest") rather than myself (my every instinct told me to manipulate the situation rather than to behave like an adult) actually worked. And it was only at that point that it occurred to me that maybe Elizabeth—maintaining an impressively lengthy deep freeze over something so easily rectified—was a little insane herself.

"Oh my, oh my. Pray for her," said Amy, naturally.

That's why groups are my higher power. We make better decisions together than we do alone; we are better at life together than we are alone. Addicts often don't acquire normal life skills. We have to practice those things that come innately to most: behaving like adults, paying our own way in life, doing the right thing instead of the easy thing, and being honest. The good news is that, with practice, I hear those traits can become instinctive. But, until then, I've got help: the Wolf Pack, a large group of life-skills-challenged, twelve-stepping, alcoholic friends.

I have long had this idea—more of a dream, really—that I could be the kind of person who wakes up at 6:30 every morning, runs, does yoga, meditates, writes a novel, goes to work, and eats healthily. But for all of my life, I have set the alarm and failed. As much as I hoped sobriety would magically transform me into a morning person, my brain still makes a break for Crazy Town every time the alarm rings out (*I don't really need to get up right now, I had a bad dream and I deserve more rest, jogging is totally supposed to happen tomorrow. In fact, I think I feel a tickle in my throat; I'm clearly too sick to jog*). My friend Ashley Anne has the same problem. A native Texan turned D.C. public-school teacher, Ashley Anne has to be at work by 7:30, a time she, much like myself, finds unholy. Enter Jim. Jim, a charming midwesterner with a wonderful eye for the absurd, has a terrible money situation (hello, he's an alcoholic)—unpaid taxes, foreclosures, creditors' phone calls, bankruptcy, even a dead accountant—and he needs to spend at least ten minutes every morning doing some paperwork. But he won't do it. The Tax Issue has become his Sisyphean task—much like rising at dawn has become mine and Ashley Anne's. But Jim is a morning person.

"Girl, get your feet on the floor, and go put your expression on!" Jim says to Ashley Anne every morning at six when he gives her a wake-up call.

"Riiise and shiiine, it's a new day," Ashley Anne purrs into the phone when I answer at 6:30, her gorgeous drawl making each word ten syllables.

"Fuck, it's early," I reply every single morning. Sometimes Ashley Anne even makes me turn on the faucet to prove I have left the bed and walked into another room.

And, at night, I touch base with Jim to make sure he has made some progress on his paperwork.

"Hello, Citizen! How are your taxes?"

And the circle of life continues.

These days, I have fallen out of the phone tree in a big way, ignoring the phone—or turning it off—and rolling over. But I ran a lot more this year than I did last year, and I know that, when I am ready to climb back into that crazy early morning space, Jim and Ashley Anne will be there to shame me into compliance. It's amazing how quickly, creatively, and thoughtfully people will respond if I just ask for help when I need it. Now I just call on the Wolf Pack, and I find there are as many solutions to my problems as there are people I am willing to ask. We are protective of one another and check in on one another often. Also, like wolves, we howl at the moon. (Okay, I howl at the moon. But Peter doesn't like it; he thinks it makes our dog anxious.) Alone, I am a lazy git. Together, we are powerful.

It's like bats. One night in early sobriety, during an intense nature-programming phase, I was watching *National Geographic*. A swarm of bats covered a sandy cliff wall, undulating and shifting together as they scoured the precipice for food. Meanwhile, large birds of prey would occasionally pass by and pluck a bat from its fellows. The most vulnerable bats were those off to the side or alone. And I thought that these bats had singularly empty lives. The size of the swarm

ensured that most bats would live and perpetuate more bats—
and that was more important than any one bat. Where the
swarm had power, the single bat was bird food. Where the
swarm had purpose, the single bat was hollow. *Poor bat,* I
thought.

Then I saw some photographs of an event on the National Mall. There we were—we conscious, unique human
beings with our innate higher intelligence and our opposable
thumbs—swarming. And why shouldn't we? The more per-
spectives we seek, the more people we encounter, the greater
our chances at success. Alone, we may not even know what
questions to ask.

Now, when I talk to H.P., I always say I'm thankful for
my Pack.

The night I tried to say my first prayer, the same night
I ended up rocking on my heels in the corner contemplating just how alone we all are floating out here in space by
ourselves, I didn't yet have the Wolf Pack. Or, I should say,
I didn't know I had them. I just knew that a creature such
as myself seemed insignificant in a universe as infinite as
ours. I wondered how my sobriety could matter that much;
I wondered how a prayer—hushed words in a dim room—
could matter at all. But maybe I could act "as if" like Amy
said—as if all of it mattered, as if the awe of the girl who
saw the moon man could be recaptured, as if just being
open to wonder could lead to inner enlightenment. And, as

Unwasted

I reflected on the odds of humanity emerging in the loneliness of outer space, how could I not have awe? After all, first there was nothing, there was just endless nothing, and now there are moral animals who live in cities that make *Blade Runner* look dated, who can read Dante, photograph supernovas, breed orchids, and listen to the Violent Femmes on the weekends. We fall in love and weep at beauty; we suffer heartbreak and wound one another mercilessly. We study physics, literature, nutrition, architecture, biology; we study ourselves, psychology, the brain; we study quantum physics and realize that, like the universe, we, too, are more nothing than we are something. We are composed of trillions of dancing motes fashioned to look like people; we are whirling dervishes constantly diving into the cool waters of the unknown. It's so easy to be hyper-rational, to dismiss the supernatural "God" and sneer at magical thinking. But what the hell is the universe if not an insane act of magic?

So does the grand magician wear long robes and twirl the end of his white beard in a gnarled finger while keeping score of our good deeds and bad? Doubtful. But does God have a consciousness? It must—because we simple humans do. By definition, a higher power would at least have what we mere mortals do. And that's pretty hard for me to conceive. But maybe it's a kind of evolved consciousness that defies human logic and language. Perhaps God is just an intensely potent force comprised of dark matter that existed before the universe, that has always just existed. That higher power may not require my worship nor care if little old Sacha drinks or not; that higher power cruises by Planet Earth on its celestial way while good things happen to bad people and really horrible things happen to truly wonderful people. That God may not be worth my worship, but maybe it is worth getting to know. Maybe when I try to talk to this galactic power surge, I, too, become more powerful, more energized, more peaceful. After all, people of faith live longer than those without it, meditation reduces disease indicators and stress, and patients who pray recover faster than those who don't. Perhaps the energy of the universe, the tide along which we all roll, is worth at least thinking over. Perhaps prayer, meditation, chanting, and ritual are all just ways of honing the ham radios of our minds and tuning in.

Besides there are some things I do have faith in. I have faith that there is a scientific explanation for just about everything; maybe, for example, human beings appear to be relative solids instead of swirling and transient particles as a defense mechanism that prevents our brains from exploding. And I have faith that every scientific explanation will be matched by a new mystery of the universe that needs unraveling. And I have faith that the more science reveals, the more in awe of the world I will be. The more science shows us about the electric-rainbow-light-show creatures that occupy the blackest recesses of the ocean, the more light the Hubble telescope throws on the deepest nights, the more we tunnel into the enigmas of the human brain, the more in awe of the universe I am. Maybe in the absence of a personal faith in God, I can, in fact, act "as if." As if the higher powers of the universe are worth addressing even if they don't really hear me. As if I were the kind of person who gets up early and goes running. As if I were a writer who did not procrastinate by watching reality-TV marathons on Bravo and then hated herself in the morning. As if I were a person who didn't drink. I just don't drink. No matter what.

I don't have God, but I have awe. I watch the ceiling in my bedroom lift off and go black until I see the place where stars and spacemen lurk, where the man on the moon watches over me. I don't have ultimate faith, but through a trick of DNA and evolution I am conscious. And, with that consciousness, I marvel. I notice the majesty. The expanding, unfolding, unfathomable universe. Perhaps that is all prayer is: noticing the majesty. Inadequately, I call the unanswerable question "H.P." and I try to talk to it most nights. And I go to twelve-step meetings regularly to remind myself of my new code of ethics, my new principles for living: rigorous honesty, humility, and an examined life. Also, I have boots on the ground: a Wolf Pack behind me at all times. That group wisdom is itself a kind of spirituality. I may not have found God, but I found something higher than myself, and I was able to retain some of that moon-man awe I experienced as a little girl.

Number 7 on the Sacha Fantasy Relapse Pass: Aliens

When aliens from the Galaxy Spiritum take over Planet Earth, the human race is thrown into turmoil. Fear and panic rule the streets as Earthlings cower beneath the massive flying saucers hovering above every major world city. Bars and pubs across the world fill with scared humans—drinking cosmos-politans and Mar(tian)tinis—on a last bender before what is surely the end of the world. But I resist. I fight the urge to drink, trusting that I will need my wits about me when the aliens make their intentions clear. Whether the extra terrestrials are here to make peace or to colonize the planet by sucking our brains out of our ears, I will face my fate nobly: clean and sober.

Soon the chief Galaxy Spiritum envoys, Grog and Mead, set up a temporary alien government in the AARP building on E Street in Northwest Washington, D.C., and prepare to address the nation.

"Greetings, Earthlings," begins Grog, the chattier of the two alien emissaries, in a resounding baritone. "We come in peace on a simple research mission."

Mead nods along, quietly adding, "We are graduate students."

Grog continues, "We are the authors of the Alien

Alcohol Research Project. We will be drafting several thousand native Earthlings from across the planet to serve as test subjects for our thesis: 'The Deleterious Effects of Forced Alien Relapse on Alcoholic Humanoids.' "

"We're 'All But Dissertation,' " *Mead says apologetically.*

"Compliance is absolute!" yells Grog suddenly. "We have ray guns."

And, with that, television screens across the globe go dark. I turn to Peter and say, "What are the odds—" when we hear a sharp knock at the door.

A few weeks later:

"Gee, hon'," says Peter as he walks into the apartment after a long day of work and notices me sprawled on the couch wearing a tinfoil hat and surrounded by empty bottles, pizza boxes, a hot glue gun, and piles of glitter. "I just hate that you've been conscripted into the Alien Alcohol Research Project. I can't imagine how hard this must be for you."

"It's hell," I say. "And, unfortunately, I'm going to need another vodka tonic."

"Let me get it for you, babe," says Peter. "Poor thing." I try to hand him the rocketship sculpture I've made for him that afternoon, but a pizza box is cemented to my left hand and I fear I will lose purchase on the couch if I try to move.

Sacha Z. Scoblic

"I'm just glad the aliens let me live—oh! Don't forget the lime."

Meanwhile, in downtown Washington, D.C., Grog and Mead are watching on a closed-circuit television and taking notes.

"Why does she think the tinfoil hat will protect her?" asks Mead.

"I don't know," says Grog, "but I think it's time to suck her brain out of her ear."

Chapter 8

Working Through It

ometimes I know I've made progress in my recovery by what I *don't* do. Recently, when a colleague told me how interesting it is that people have different levels of addiction, I didn't go bat shit. Nathan, who had just finished reading a little *Infinite Jest* and was therefore now somewhat versed in twelve-step culture, was probably just trying to connect with me in his own way. Even though any amateur expert should probably know to steer clear of certain anonymous organizations in conversation, I let it go. After all, I had long since published articles about my own struggle with the bottle; I was out of the closet as an addict. I was fair game.

"Levels of addiction?" I ask.

"I mean," Nathan says, "it's not like you're some hard-core tattooed person."

As if there lay the Rubicon. As if our addictions are

measured by our appearances. But then, didn't I also think just that when I first got clean? I wondered where my punk-rockers and scenesters were when I sat down at my first twelve-step meeting next to a lobbyist. I was stunned by what an idiot I had been back then and thought suddenly of Caitlyn, the suburban soccer mom in khakis and a pastel scrunchie who once stripped for crack, or Esther, the well-to-do Georgetown dame who looks like a librarian and was currently still drinking herself to death in her $3 million town house. No tats. Hard core. Occasionally at a twelve-step meeting, I do see the tattoo of wild youth peeking out from the lawyer's blouse or on the neck of an administrative assistant as she brushes aside her hair. Conversely, I often see the straight-edge chick with the sleeve tattoos and piercings who quit drugs and alcohol at eighteen after senior year got out of hand and is now pursuing her Ph.D. in sociology when she isn't meditating. As is usually the case in life, labels are useless. "Hard-core tattooed" people don't have a monopoly on this disease any more than do town drunks, stepparents, barflies, lawyers, or ne'er-do-wells. And the thing about recovery is that a lot of those formerly hard-core types abandon the attention-drawing behavior for quieter, more authentic lives in mom jeans and tote bags. Then there's my dear friend Rachel, who celebrates her sober life *avec* tattoos, including a brand-new giant lioness on her calf.

And though all of this was floating through my head begging for me to impose some kind of order on it, I just looked at Nathan and saw the phrase "it's not like you're some hard-core tattooed person" just stuck out there twinkling in midair, begging me to enter the fray. And, though a small voice inside me whispered, *It's a trap! It's a trap!*, I heard myself say:

"I do, too, have tattoos."

When people don't like me, this is why, I thought to myself: I'd rather subvert Nathan's assumption—an assumption (cough, cough) that I used to share—than actually engage him in a meaningful dialogue about any of this. And, what's worse: I have *a* tattoo, singular; not the bevy of secret tattoos I had just implied. I guess if I'm going to get nasty and subvert idiotic expectations, I might as well go down swinging.

"Yes," Nathan says rather comfortably, as though he knows all about these tattoos of mine, which he most certainly does not—either because they do not, heh, exist or because my one lone tattoo rests discreetly on my hip, where no colleague has been invited. "But"—Nathan continues smiling mischievously—"do you remember getting them?"

And I stop. Right there, I stop. And I force myself not to invent some lurid story about the skull-and-crossbones tats I got in a blackout, when, in truth, I got a rose tattoo in homage to Tennessee Williams one bright sunny day while living abroad and not at all drunk. I force myself to stop taking the bait—bait I alone am imagining, no doubt. I force myself to remember that Nathan has been very good to me, that Nathan is exactly the kind of colleague you want on your team when you start to slip under alcoholic waters. He has been especially good to me when we travel.

My sobriety is most vulnerable when I am out of town with colleagues—as opposed to friends and confidantes. Not only am I surrounded by coworkers eager to melt the awkward facade of office pseudo-friendship with cocktails, I am sealed into a hotel room with a mini-bar and left utterly to my own devices. Alone in a hotel room, I am acutely aware that no one is looking at anything I am doing—except perhaps the expertly neutral eyes of the hotel clerk as she explains the complex litany of "refreshment" charges on my bill. One advantage of being open about my addiction at work is that everyone is aware that I won't be drinking. I guess it's doubtful that anyone would body-tackle me, slamming a drink in my hand to the ground before I had a sip; they would more likely raise their eyebrows and discuss what to do behind my back. But I'd rather not be subject to either reaction. Though, come to think of it, I should say it is doubtful that anyone would body-tackle me *except Nathan.* Nathan would lie down in traffic for me if it seemed important; not out of any abiding allegiance to me, but more due to an almost irrational enthusiasm for helping out anyone he cares about or knows—and probably strangers, too, for that matter. Still, alone in a hotel room, I am tantalizingly unsupervised.

Which is why business trips require a measure of fortitude and psychic energy not required on normal days. I must be devoted to my defenses: Am I tired? Hungry? Frustrated?

Homesick? Any chink in my armor can lead to a complete meltdown. I prefer to bathe my feelings in copious amounts of alcohol rather than feel them. So now, still an infant in my sobriety, when forced to encounter my own feelings, I am ill-equipped to deal with them and can perceive situations that most adults might find merely annoying to be soul-sucking nightmares from which I must escape. On one particularly rough business trip with Nathan and our colleague Jen, I spun out of control at an impromptu cocktail party.

After spending twelve-hour days reporting on every session of a conference that lasted three days, I was fried. In celebration of the end of this marathon of seminars, the plan was to eat a lot of Mexican food and get very drunk. Though I didn't intend to drink, being in a setting outside of the conference hall and surrounded by food sounded pretty perfect to me. But then, a funny thing happened: No one left the conference hall. Bolstered by all of the leftover wine from the confab, my colleagues *milled.* They drank and mingled and ambled and did something I didn't think possible: They actually devised a way to party in slow motion. Each sip of wine gave them pleasure for what seemed like hours—it satiated their hunger, gave the antiseptic conference hall a kind of warm glow, and the part of their brains that was exhausted was blocked from consciousness. It was super-wine.

As they moved like tortoises in no rush at all to depart, I grew edgy. I was not drinking the magic wine; I was still in real time, struggling with my groaning stomach, the migraine-inducing fluorescent lighting, and the deep, deep desire to make it back to my hotel room early enough to watch a movie in bed. The more people assured me we'd leave soon ("after this glass of wine"), the more languid the vibe became. Here's the thing about people: They don't do what you want when you want them to. Even when you really, really want them to. I considered just leaving on my own, of course. But I was concerned that would make too much of a statement: SENSITIVE ALCOHOLIC CHICK STORMS OUT! Besides, the rental-car logistics were complex; I was relying on these slow-sipping sops to shepherd me out of there. And as I watched them all nursing their drinks, I thought, *I am never getting away. I am totally trapped.*

My eyes welled up with tears. *Oh no. Oh no. Fuck. Fuck. Fuck. Don't cry. Don't cry.* I made it to the bathroom before my emotions exploded out of my eyelids in an involuntary burst. I told myself to get it together. I gave myself a stern talking-to. *I will not cry at work. I will not cry at work.* But the dam had broken. I was on the verge of hyperventilating when Jen walked in.

"I'm fine," I said immediately when she looked at me startled and concerned. "There's just a lot of booze out there," I said, preferring to keep the explanation simple rather than admitting that everyone was too slow and that, if they were going to drink, I was going to need some food and a change of scene stat.

"What can I get you?" asked Jen so sweetly, so dulcetly, I thought I might hug her, which made me cry more. At this point, I probably had salt deposits at my feet.

"Oh, I'll be fine," I continued despite massive physical evidence to the contrary. "This isn't your fight; I can do this," I said in a faux-tough voice, like this had happened a thousand times before and I was battle-weary. Which, in retrospect, just made me sound even more pathetic.

I was four years into sobriety, and I could still be brought to my knees by a few colleagues and a few cocktails.

* * *

In that moment, it was as though no time had passed without alcohol at all, as though I were still six months sober and heading to my first corporate retreat—a horrible event I remembered all too well. At six months sober, any encounter with alcohol could bring me to my knees. Luckily, for most of my first year clean, sobriety had been a private affair—an affair between the couch, the television, and me. Then the *Reader's Digest* retreat rolled around, and I realized how vulnerable I was whenever I left the office or my apartment.

The retreat was really just an awkward weekend for senior staff at the *Digest*'s editorial corporate consultant's home in the Hamptons. The *Digest* hired Kate to run focus groups on everything from cover colors to potential headlines. Kate's house was built in the 1980s and was an imitation of the famously charming, gray, shingled Hamptons manses one finds covered in hydrangea at the end of a bluff or snuggled into a dune out on the island. But the imitation was imperfect. More McMansion than manse, the home was a little too straight, a little too conventional, and manicured so completely as to be indistinguishable from a 5,000-square-foot home in suburban Indianapolis. Not a wildflower, speck of sand, or blade of beach grass in sight. The grass that was present was golf-course neat, a crew cut of a lawn that had probably never actually been set foot on. No lazy star-gazing, picnicking, or touch football on this yard; like good china, plastic furniture covers, and artfully groomed toy poodles, this grass was meant to be gazed upon and preserved—not touched or used.

My first time there had also been a cool six months before I quit drinking. I found Kate at central command in the kitchen, dicing mint for welcome Mojitos and yelling out room assignments. I threw back a Mojito, grabbed another, and wandered upstairs to find myself in Kate's college-age daughter's room. I glanced at the bathroom I'd be sharing with all of my female colleagues, resented the male coworkers for being assigned rooms at the bed-and-breakfast in town, sighed, and sped downstairs again when Kate shouted, "Who wants more Mojitos?!" I was a decade younger than everyone at the retreat, but when you take people away from their families and responsibilities for a night, they make up for lost time. We all drank like fish, ate everything in Kate's kitchen, and sang karaoke until well past midnight. Then I spent the wee hours of the evening sitting by Kate's pool and listening to the embarrassing confessions of my colleague Dina, an attractive fifty-something with a chic, jet-black hairdo and slightly more edge than most people were comfortable with at the *Digest*. I found her a little odd in that kooky cat-lady, is-she-or-isn't-she-a-Wiccan kind of way, but ultimately harmless.

"You've got to wonder about a man who's sixty and never been married," she said, eyebrows raised.

"Have you ever been married?" I asked.

"It's different for women," she assured me before continuing her lecture on the pitfalls of Match.com. "So anyway, my latest Internet date warned me he likes to spank," Dina said. And, at the same moment that I said, "Hot," she said, "Gross, right?"

It all ended with awkward glances around the breakfast table.

The only work I recall being accomplished was a post-breakfast "download" in which we were all supposed to pass around our favorite magazines—not including the *Digest*, natch—and explain what unique qualities it had from which we writers and editors could learn. Almost every woman brought a copy of *O*, the Oprah magazine, while the male editors all seemed to read *Business Week*—not coincidentally, the magazine where Kate's husband worked. One poor guy brought *Rock and Gem* magazine, and you could see Kate mentally rolling her eyes. Having neglected to do the assignment at all, I made a Hail Mary pass.

"I don't have a magazine today, because I no longer read magazines," I said dramatically. "I get all my articles *online*," I continued, as though it were 1998. It was, I thought, a clever ploy that had the added advantage of being mostly true.

"That's just the kind of fresh thinking we need!" exclaimed Kate while someone passed me a copy of *O*.

This moment was a decent metaphor for my career at the *Digest*: I was excellent at deferring work I didn't want to do until the last possible moment and then pulling something surprisingly successful out of the clear blue sky. After doing work that I did enjoy doing—say, finishing an article—I would give myself permission to take a day or two off from actually committing any further acts of work while still in the office sitting perched at my desk trolling the Internet as a reward for doing exactly what I was supposed to have done to begin with; that is, my job. Also, I liked to take a full day off away from the office every few weeks—a clever mix of vacation days, personal days for nonexistent emergencies and nonexistent deaths in the family (which always made me feel *almost* guilty enough not to use it as an excuse), and fake sick days. I was failing upward.

Kate concluded the "download" session and the weekend by asking us to detail on paper in list form precisely which linens we had used (from sheets to towels) that weekend, affix

that list to one of our used pillowcases, and then fill said pil-
lowcase with the contents of the list. I grabbed a secret to-go
Mojito, stripped my bed, and stole someone's copy of *O* for
the train.

So, a year later, when the next *Digest* office retreat rolled
around, I knew what kind of strange brew to expect. Only,
this time, I was six months sober and still assiduously avoid-
ing heavy-drinking events just like this one. But Kate had
made it clear that attendance was mandatory—that is, an
awkward weekend at Kate's stridently neat house in the
Hamptons during which no work would actually get done
was a compulsory job function. Not only would I be trapped
with middle-aged suburbanites cutting loose, I would have
to act like a "team player" the whole time. Desperately fear-
ing for my sobriety, I hatched a plan. I would tell kooky,
repulsed-by-spanking Dina that I was a newly sober alcoholic and ask her for discretion before we headed out to Long
Island. I needed to have at least one person at the retreat
who knew I didn't drink; it was an insurance policy that I at
least wouldn't drink in front of Dina. Kind of like when you
tell everyone you know that you are off sugar (because that
sounds like a healthy lifestyle choice instead of just saying
you feel like a cow and need to lose weight), ask all of your
friends to keep you honest about it, die inside while everyone
around you eats chocolate birthday cake, and then binge on
Oreos by yourself later that night. I was hoping it would work

something like that—without the bingeing. Dina would keep me honest, if only for the night.

"Of course," said Dina, when I revealed my plan. "I should cut down, too. You know these weekends are so absurd. It's like a frat party."

I immediately relaxed: Dina got it. And so, I didn't get too uptight when she began digging for all the dirty details ("Did you hit a really rough bottom?" she asked, while I commanded myself not to make a spanking joke).

Right away Kate noticed I wasn't drinking and punished me by making me shuck corn while she blended margaritas.

"So that's it then," she said to me. "No booze for you this weekend?"

"Nope," I replied as though it were indeed just about this weekend.

Kate sighed and then yelled, "Who wants a margarita?!"

Throughout the night, Dina would approach me, squeeze my shoulder, look meaningfully at me, and ask, "Are you doing okay with everything?" But I wasn't complaining; she was taking her role seriously and, it seemed, sincerely. I appreciated her concern. Especially after my colleague Renita looked at me coolly across the dinner table, nodded to my empty wineglass, and said in a voice sure to be heard throughout the house, "Oh, I get it. You're pregnant."

"No," I replied. "I'm just a proud Jehovah's Witness."

Renita laughed and let it go, just as Kate yelled, "Who's in for tequila and poker?!"

Despite Dina's enthusiasm for my sobriety (she had be-
gun to catch my eye and then silently mouth the words "You
okay?" from across the room as though I were being forced
to watch my sweetheart make out with my mortal enemy),
I ultimately white-knuckled it through the whole night, dying inside when everyone started draining the tequila bottle.
Watching people sip wine at dinner is one thing; watching
people drink to get drunk is another. Every sip seemed like
a lurid, slow-motion act. I watched as my colleagues licked
poison from their lips and slurred, as they made sloppy toasts
and flung the liquor back, eyes wide, brains flickering out. It
looked almost graphic, or X-rated. I saw one coworker throw
back whiskey with relish, and I felt as though I might as well
be seeing him shoot up heroin, slice off a finger with a but-
ter knife, and jerk off onto the dining room table. The room
started spinning, and I watched as my colleagues turned into
the Lizard People of Hunter S. Thompson's hallucinations
right before my eyes—crazed, booze-soaked reptiles with
huge jaws and evil laughs. Fuck, I quit using in part to avoid
horror-show visions like this. I wanted to run and cry.

As much as I liked Kate, I pledged I would not return for
the office retreat in the Hamptons the following year.

Back at the office, the *Digest* went back to normal: My
colleagues stopped looking like lizard people and returned
their attentions to the next miracle baby, shark attack, or
angel sighting they could find. But I never forgot that Dina
had nobly tried to protect me from myself, and I welcomed

177

the opportunity to write a short column about environmentally savvy products for her. But Dina was hard to please. After I brought her a list of websites for heritage turkeys and organic table linens for Thanksgiving, she chastised me for succumbing to a theme. "We don't want the column to be so matchy-matchy with the season," she said with a dramatic sigh of exasperation; I swear she almost said, "Duh, Sacha." And yet, when I brought her a list of products in December, she agitated for more holiday items and designed the page in the shape of—wait for it—a Christmas tree. Let's just say it was über matchy-matchy. Despite these setbacks between us, when Dina asked me to endorse eco-friendly wine in my next column, I felt confident she'd understand when I demurred. I just couldn't stomach telling a huge audience of people to buy alcohol—let alone recommending alcohol I hadn't so much as tasted and never would. And while suggesting or not suggesting a winery didn't feel like the kind of meaningful issue I particularly wanted to take a moral stand on, the more I thought about signing my name to this endorsement, the more uncomfortable I became. Ultimately, since the wine part of the column was just going to be a quick mention, I felt sure Dina wouldn't mind if I passed. In fact, I thought Dina might write a sentence about the winery herself or just scrap the item and call it a day.

I was wrong. The next thing I knew, Dina was yelling at me in front of another editor. I couldn't fathom the fury she had mustered; clearly, I had missed the nuances of when to go thematic and when not to. But this seemed like a bigger problem and Dina railed on. She said I had no right to refuse an assignment and that she'd thought about it, and it was perfectly fair to ask me to write about wine because it's not her fault I was an alcoholic, and it's not like I had a religious excuse; it's not like I was "a Mormon or anything." Indeed. In that moment, everything stopped; a wall of silence slammed against my face, and I was left stunned and shaking. I couldn't immediately reconcile what was happening, but I knew I had just been dealt a low blow (*"It's not my fault you're an alcoholic," "It's not like you're a Mormon or anything"*). When the yelling subsided, I climbed down under my desk and cried with all the fury and emotion that months of hard-fought sobriety had left me drowning in. When would this get easier? Why was my colleague insane?

I was devastated by Dina's betrayal of my trust. That she had so casually thrown the word *alcoholic* around in front of another colleague stung, but that she had used my secret as a weapon against me felt unforgivable. I thought about calling human resources that day as I sat under my desk, basking in the anger of the righteous and the self-pity of the wronged, and weeping for myself, a woman who could no longer drink over this bit of cruelty and then forget it ever happened. But I didn't call human resources; instead, I went home to Peter and created a responsible exit strategy. I may have been a simpering alcoholic, but I also wasn't happy at the *Digest*. When one is actively planning how not to do work, perhaps one is in the wrong gig. And while I may have been eager to leave, the larger truth is that the *Digest* also deserved a much better employee than I could give them at that time.

* * *

So, with four years sober, as I stood in front of Jen in the bathroom of the conference hall mid-hysteria, all I could think was: *This is fucking ridiculous. I have got to stop crying at work!* And, just as I was explaining to Jen how totally fine I was—voice quivering, eyes blinking—my phone buzzed. Nathan had texted me to see if I was okay. He was there if I needed him. As though prompted, Jen looked at me and said the most beautiful words:

"You know, Sacha, I'm not just your colleague; I'm your friend."

And that was it. I exhaled and pulled myself together. I knew Jen and Nathan would never throw it in my face that I was an alcoholic; they were crossover hits: colleagues who are also friends. While I washed up, Jen and Nathan made plans for a small quiet dinner at a restaurant that would not be the scene of a post-conference party. I left the bathroom and walked through the hall looking more like a dead bunny rabbit than a human being and, goddamn it, left the conference hall and got some food.

Nathan and Jen have never made anything out of my alcoholism. And, though I was concerned that the legacy of that business trip would be that my colleagues would now make ultra-secret, don't-tell-Sacha bar outings whenever I was around or try not to drink in front of me, that has never been the case (as far as I know!). I am invited along on just about every excursion no matter how boozy, and mostly I can handle it—though when everyone starts doing shots, slurring their words, or doing the hazy drunk sway, I still have to leave. I don't want to be there when the lizard people come out. And, when I see the reptilian skin oozing out from under a polo shirt, I still kind of shut down and wonder when all of this will stop bothering me so much. Nevertheless, having calmly sat through more rounds of cocktails with my co-workers than I would have believed possible just a few years ago, I am always aware that I will be okay. Unlike with Dina and even Kate, I feel safe with these crossover stars. And I always have my Wolf Pack standing there beside me.

For as many drinking opportunities as my job provides, I feel pretty good about continually chatting up colleagues and conference attendees with a bright smile, a reservoir of psychic energy I muster for such occasions, and a solid exit strategy. But I am sure that, among the colleagues who know what I am, when I say something reactive, when I get tense, or when I disagree, I am instantly the woman with issues instead of the woman simply having a bad day. I'm the office alcoholic.

And so, when I heard Nathan drop phrases like "levels of

addiction" and "it's not like you're some hard-core tattooed person," I did not freak out on him. But I did behave hastily, thoughtlessly, and untruthfully. I bartered my integrity for my pride.

"I do too have tattoos."

"Yes," says Nathan. "But do you remember getting them?"

Like I said, I stopped right there. Remembering or not remembering a tattoo is not a yardstick. I will not tell him about the really ugly stuff, the stuff that would make this tattoo business look like child's play, like the morning after an Ecstasy-fueled club night when this lone-tattoo-having, Banana Republic-wearing, freshly highlighted blonde spiraled into a ketamine-induced abyss so deep I developed magnifying-glass eyes and could see every blade of tobacco in my cigarette before flying into outer space and watching myself in my friend's living room from far above while Earthbound me apparently had a normal conversation with the people around her. I will not mention that to Nathan. I will not one-up or last-word him. Because, even if my bottom were lily-white, even if I had gently come clean after a quiet epiphany one morning over aspirin and a glass of water, my addiction is as real and alive as anyone's. And the moment I start thinking that I have a different level of addiction, that I am not so hard-core, that's the moment I will decide I can handle a drink after all. Sure, there are folks in recovery—

and out—whose lives make mine look like *Muppet Babies.*
But I know their hunger, I know their sense of urgency, I
know their manipulative and wily ways. Our stories are different; our disease is the same. And so I just stopped myself
from sparring with Nathan. And I thought about my Wolf
Pack, a silent army standing behind me who has never once
made me feel less of an addict. It is no wonder James Frey felt
he had to lie and embellish in *A Million Little Pieces;* everybody these days seems to think you aren't yet a real addict
until you've shot a man for crack, drank until your eyes bled,
and swaddled yourself in tattoos. But there's no competition
to see who is more or less of an addict; because in a very fun-
damental way, we are all the same. My disease is the same
as every addict's, even the shotgun-toting, eye-bleeding, tattooed crackhead alcoholic. I just stopped sooner. Hopefully,
I will never find out how much farther down the rabbit hole
I might have gone. And so Nathan made me realize that it is
phrases like "levels of addiction" that make it hard for some
of us to come into recovery early. *I am not an alcoholic, because I have a job! I am not an alcoholic, because I have a
mortgage! I am not an alcoholic, because I don't look like
the people on* Intervention." We think we haven't reached
the lowest levels of addiction yet; and we think we have to
be face-down in the gutter before we can call ourselves addicts. Today, I am so grateful that I stopped comparing myself with other peoples' levels of addiction and just looked at

the mess before me and came in from the storm. What kind of alcoholic am I? What level? The one where you can never drink again.

While Nathan buzzes around the room, I recall his protective arm around the shoulders of the dead-bunny-rabbit-faced girl he accompanied out of the conference hall. I recall his constant appraisals of me at office events ("I've got the car, we can leave any time"). I recall my initial impression of this conversation: that Nathan was reading a book about addicts and was attempting—no doubt now with regrets—to connect with me.

I smile and laugh. "I guess I'm not a hard-core tattooed person." And then I let it go.

Number 8 on the Sacha Fantasy Relapse Pass: Superpower

It's true that I bought the little lamp on a trip through the Middle East specifically because I thought it looked like something that when rubbed would emit a genie. I've been told I look a little like Barbara Eden from I Dream of Jeannie, *and I have a soft spot for little golden lamps and lanterns. But I certainly never imagined that my newly acquired lamp would actually contain a genie. After all, just because one purchases a golden lantern does not mean one experiments with*

*crudely rubbing said lantern to and fro. I might never
have discovered the genie at all but for a small dusting
accident—wherein I knocked the lamp from its perch on
my bookshelf and sort of bobbled it from hand to hand in
an attempt to keep from dropping it to the floor. The action must have created the necessary friction, and, well,
here we are.*

*"Master," says a breathless blonde in sheer scarves from
out of a kind of smoky haze emanating from the lamp.*

*At first, I assume that whatever dust I dislodged from
the ancient lantern must have included some opium.*

*"I am not a hallucination, master," says the genie, ob-
viously a telepath.*

*Oh no! A telepath! I'm going to end up wishing for the
Stay Puft Marshmallow Man and regretting it!*

*"I don't grant wishes," says the genie. "But I can give
you one superpower of your choice. Take your time."*

*"What kind of a genie grants superpowers?" I ask. "I
mean, the golden lamp, the belly ring, you're so authentic, I would think this would be a classic three-wishes
type of scenario."*

*"Are you going to argue with the superpower genie?
Should I go back to sleep for a thousand years?"*

Right.

*I of course consider the obvious choices: flying, clair-
voyance, invisibility. But it doesn't take long before it
hits me.*

"The choice has been made," says the genie as she is whisked back into the lamp by forces stranger than I care to dwell upon.

It isn't until my next business trip that I am sure my wish has come true.

* * *

The minibar sits patiently, waiting good-naturedly as I explore the granite bathroom, open the door to the small patio and take a deep breath of cool air, and run my fingers along the Frette comforter. The minibar is brimming with delicious warm ambers and chilled golds. The ice bucket is already full. A small crystal goblet sits next to it; a card is tucked inside. It reads, "USE THIS! LOVE, GENIE."

Something about hotel rooms, especially beautiful hotel rooms, always makes me feel as though the rules have been suspended. Whether I am one hundred or one thousand miles from home, hotel rooms exist out of time or place. They are secret chambers drifting outside of normal life. It's like the way foreign currency just feels like Monopoly money; a good hotel room makes you feel like you're playing a great game of make-believe, like nothing you do is really happening.

And so, I head toward the minibar.

And it's totally okay: I have a special no-consequences hotel-minibar superpower. Bad. Ass.

Chapter 9

Midnight Demons

"You cannot dance to Led Zeppelin!" Nick laughed. "No one can dance to Zeppelin! It's impossible." But I heard a challenge—and the opening chords to "Immigrant Song." Thrusting myself in small fits like a sexy ten-year-old with palsy, I single-mindedly searched for an elusive beat I could dance to in between cigarette breaks and Cape Cods. That was the last time I drank on New Year's Eve, the last night of 2004, a night that is—to my eternal horror—captured on a digital recorder and seen by, I swear, everyone Nick has ever met.

New Year's Eve has gone from being my favorite holiday—unabashed drunkenness, with glittery hats and noise-makers—to being my least favorite. It used to be that New Year's Eve meant leaving behind the pressures of holiday gift-giving and escaping the expectations of family for the rollicking promise of a party. It was a night that made my desires normal, that evened the scales between my behavior and the world's. Kind of like how freaks and malcontents can blend in on Halloween, New Year's Eve brought the world to my doorstep. *Welcome, my pretties. Now we can all fetishize alcohol together.* New Year's Eve was a great equalizer.

Without alcohol, New Year's Eve is very hard to love—particularly because everyone else does have alcohol and the one night that made me as sane as the rest of the world now shuts me out entirely. Not only do I have my now usual hallucinations of lizard people when I see friends downing shots and slinging back champagne like it's ice water on a hot day, I have the uncomfortable internal dissonance of both wanting to flee and to spend time with them—after all, they are my friends, and often the very friends I only see but once a year. Sometimes New Year's Eve feels like some kind of horrible alcoholic penance wherein I must atone for years of wasted holidays by bearing witness to the debauchery of the night, acting as a designated driver, and tolerating the ill-conceived drunken confidences of my comrades.

"How long have you been sober now? I respect what you are doing sooo much," slurred my friend Jaye a few New Year's Eves ago, hovering uncomfortably close to my face, her champagne testing the limits of its flute. Irony, sadly, is lost on the drunk. "Is it like quitting smoking? Is the craving just always there?"

I get this a lot. Indeed, that very night, Peter and I had

gone in on a pack of cigarettes together though we had quit ages before. Sometimes, if I must be surrounded by vice, then, hell, I want one of my own. I suppose it says something that ammonia-laden, nicotine-fueled, disease-packing, lethal cigarettes play a distant second to drugs and alcohol in my through-the-looking-glass world order. But I know what Jaye means about the cigarette craving—that unmistakable desire for a smoke after a great meal, with just the right bourbon, on a cold sidewalk with a cup of coffee, or even after watching an actor light up in a movie. And, yes, the craving for alcohol is that physically intense—the pungent, musky notes of a strong red when it is passed under my nose at a table can send my mind reeling: *Just one glass can't hurt; it would go so well with the meal.* As though I were some kind of classy sommelier who just wanted to make sure the food was fully experienced and not a crazy addict whose brain schemed to trick her into a complete relapse. *Just a sip, precious.* And I have to remember that the last time I agreed to "just one," I ended up coming home at seven in the morning. So, yes, I understand, both as a former drinker and as a former smoker, just how intense a true craving can be.

But drugs and alcohol, unlike cigarettes, have an insidious lure more powerful than the physical desire: They are mood-altering, mind-bending, brain-drenching substances that, for a while, completely change you. Oh sure, cigarettes relax you, take the edge off, make you feel cool (although, nowadays—when you can't even smoke in a bar and you're left shivering outdoors in the semipermanent haze of that evening's raft of smokers, side-stepping the legions of used spongy death sticks at your feet—can one really feel that cool smoking anymore?). But no one has ever become smarter, funnier, and better looking when smoking. Drinking, on the other hand, could change the entire course of my evening, and it could also change me. A cigarette has never given me the courage to jump on a pool table and dance. A cigarette has never made sitting in front of the television for eight hours a completely engrossing and satisfying experience. A cigarette has never taken me from desolation to euphoria, has never amassed the strength to hold back oceans of despair, to Bubble Wrap my senses against the daggers of the real world, and gently lull me into a completely new person—a person who happily cares for no one, who is responsible for nothing, and who is soothed by, and not fearful of, oblivion. A cigarette cannot do that. Otherwise, we'd have to pass laws against smoking and driving.

And so, I started to explain this to Jaye in my own hyper-articulate way ("It's, um, the same, but it is also, like, different") when I realized that, in a bizarre twist, I was on the verge of an authentic conversation. At myriad cocktail parties and work events, I often find myself dying to leave as early as possible—not because I am surrounded by or craving alcohol, but because, in the midst of so much mindless chatter and numbing small talk, I am overcome by an intense and self-diagnosed case of situational agoraphobia.

Those breezy conversational moments where I used to shine and where I used to win could now be skin-crawling interludes to be suffered through. Sobriety has given me a taste for the genuine. Which is odd, because most normal people and two-drink drinkers use alcohol to achieve a kind of authenticity, to lower their guards and inhibitions, to allow them to unabashedly pursue a meaningful conversation. And so, as I explained to Jaye the totally immersive effects of alcohol, as opposed to cigarettes, and how addiction is not just an intense craving but a complete brain rewire, I was completely aware that I was sharing an intimate moment with a drunk person. She needed champagne to get here; I needed the absence of it. And it was just as I was having this thought and wondering if perhaps there could be some weird conversational symbiosis between the drunk and the sober, when the balance of booze power tipped and Jaye abruptly exclaimed, "I love this song!" and was out of earshot faster than you can say, "Manic Monday." I was paying penance for past crimes against authenticity.

My most recent New Year's Eve experience was spent *watching* a rave. The last night of 2009 started out as a dinner party with Peter and six pals at our friend Phoebe's apartment in New York. We listened to the mix on Phoebe's iPod and ate lamb chops, roast potatoes, spinach salad, good cheese, and baguettes. I drank club soda with fresh lime and everyone else drank red wine. After dinner, we moved to the couch and listened to music and talked. But soon the girls were dancing, calling for me to join them, and I slipped into familiar and murky waters.

Dancing has long been a kind of loaded issue for me. I spent my childhood immersed in ballet lessons, pointe shoes, auditions, and leotards. I dreamed of the New York City Ballet, I dreamed of Alvin Ailey, I dreamed of Twyla Tharp. They were not reasonable dreams. By the time I accepted the cruel reality of my limited talent and of attending college versus joining a ballet company, I was still mourning the dream: Everyone says you can be anything you want to be in this country if you work hard enough; that is a national lie.

At first, I thought I might be able to become a dance major and still go on to pursue a modern dance career—modern dance being far less hung up on age and physical perfection and instead emphasizing personality and athleticism. But, by then, I had come to believe at the hands of my primary dance instructor—a woman who made Debbie Allen from *Fame* look like Mother Teresa—that real dancers don't go to college (also, I know now, a lie); they dance, goddamn it. And so, I figured, if I were to attend college at all, the dream was dead, and I might as well go for the best education I could instead of the best dance program. After all, I still felt competitive academically even as I watched my talent for dance wane. When I matriculated at an Ivy League school instead of a school with a first-rate dance program, I was making a very real choice to chart a new course. I attended dance classes briefly in college, watching girls who had just started dancing in their teens—or even at college itself—pretend that they could earnestly become professional dancers, as though the fine arts required nothing more than lessons three days a week for four years. Coming out of a twelve-year ballet program in which I had spent every day but Sunday taking eleven classes a week and still not feeling up to snuff, I sneered at these girls. Once in the dorm elevator, a young woman stopped me, breathless. "I saw you in ballet today," she gushed. "You are so good." *Dance idiot*, I thought. I was "so good" compared with girls who took ballet to round out their violin and Italian lessons. Compared with real dancers and compared with the students back in my old dance school at home, I was perfectly mediocre. Attending dance classes sporadically at college had only served to make me a witness to my own regression. So I joined the debate team and became a philosophy major. Was I giving up, or had I merely analyzed my skill set and made the mature decision to find something I wasn't too late to be talented for? Perhaps a little of each. To this day, I find attending or discussing great dance performances bittersweet. Toni Bentley once wrote: "Inside a corseted tutu lies untold freedom." And so it is. (Indeed, alcoholism had taught me that freedom without a corset or at least some structure wasn't freedom at all—like how putting every word in bold renders nothing bold; you are just using a dark and unreadable font. In the absence of guideposts, freedom quickly turns to chaos.)

Still, over the years, I have liked to think that I can dance

better than your average bear. Certainly, I have enjoyed dancing. I have cut a rug wherever I have landed, from putting on
shows for Tessa and Jack to all-night eighties dance parties at
a kibbutz pub in Israel to bouncing, raving nights at a disco
downtown. Eschewing technique for joy, I had found a new
way to love dance: exuberant and inebriated.

But Nick's 2004 archived footage of the Led Zeppelin
challenge bothered me. Normally, if Nick had pulled out the
video for friends to see a few months after he had captured
it, I would probably have laughed the loudest and threatened
everyone present that I'd do it all over again if they weren't
nice to me. But, when I first saw the video, it was July 2005
and I was just a few weeks sober. I couldn't laugh; I could
only see a horrifying sloppy mess on the screen before me. I
saw a woman not in control of her own limbs and, honestly,
barely upright at all. I did not look like I was even enjoying
myself; I looked lost—and not lost in the music. I was totally
gone. Everyone watching the video near me was crowding
around the screen, laughing. I started to shut down. *Turn
it off. Turn it off.* I didn't see a single moment on the screen;
I saw countless moments, endless nights wasted. I saw the
woman I was trying to shed. Watching sober while people
giggled at a snapshot of Drunk Me was singularly discon-
certing. I squirmed and discovered that I no longer wanted to
be the featured act of the night.

And so, when Phoebe cooed, "Come on, Sacha, dance

with us," five years later in 2009 as we waited to ring in the New Year, I felt a familiar anxiety spread across my limbs.

Could I still dance in front of people? Could I be exuberant and sober instead of exuberant and inebriated? I peeled myself off the couch, fully aware of the lack of alcohol inside of me, frustratingly unbolstered by the enthusiasm and energy a few drinks would have given me. I felt everyone's eyes on me in a way I had never experienced: Prior to quitting drinking, I had never understood the phrase "unwanted attention." I did now—viscerally. And the dancing didn't come easy, either. Suddenly I was twelve, at my first junior-high-school dance, and very aware that the ballet moves I had studied so fervently were not going to translate into the cool factor I wanted to convey at that moment. I mean, the cute blond kid who lived down the street from me wore a silver tie at my first junior-high dance. A silver tie, people. I'm not sure it gets much cooler than that at age twelve. Twenty-some-odd years later in a low-lit apartment in New York City, there was still nothing about my sober swaying that evoked cool. (Though loving a song can help: Madonna's "Ray of Light" can whip me into a sober yet psychotic dance frenzy.)

For better or for worse, I was saved from forced dancing when it became clear the apartment below Phoebe's was having a much better party than we were. A few reconnaissance trips later and we all found ourselves amid a film-student dance party complete with an oversized screen featuring psychedelic imagery swirling about; dudes jumped up and down manically to the techno thrum in front of the screen, girls in strange wigs smoked hash on the couch, and under a coffee table a small dog ate pizza out of a box on the floor. My friends looked at each other and beamed; they had found the New Year's Eve Promised Land. But as I watched the scene before me—the clothes, the youth, the music, the art-video installation—every insecurity sobriety insists you fucking feel as you fucking feel it rushed to the surface, and I had just one persistent and overriding thought: *I am too sober for this shit.*

Just when I was maintaining friendships, nurturing a spiritual life, and finding that I didn't have to be so angry all of the time, New Year's Eve was there to show up and kick my ass. So much for the quiet New Year's Eve dinner. Penance for all the times I ditched friends for a more exciting plan.

Don't get me wrong: No one should ever have to plan around me. If I thought my friends were editing their behavior to make me, the crazy alcoholic person in the room, feel comfortable, I would feel ten times worse than I did watching them get loaded. You don't let the sickest person in the car do the driving—and you certainly don't plan an evening around their neuroses. It was New Year's Eve, for God's sake; folks are supposed to get smashed and jump around to techno music and party. It's just not ever going to be my favorite night anymore. But that's okay, because for a long time it was. And I happily relinquish that mantle in exchange for no longer compulsively planning my life around when I will get my next drink, in exchange for no more hangovers, in exchange for always remembering what I did the night before.

I noticed then that the dog eating pizza under the coffee table was also wearing a New Year's Eve hat and wondered if the hash-smoking girls were themselves wearing wigs in lieu of hats. *Maybe the dog stole their hats,* I thought, eyes narrowing.

"Let's go back upstairs, shall we?!" asked Peter brightly as he either perfectly appraised the situation or else saw the look of stark panic on my face in which I telegraphed the message: *Get me the fuck out of here before I permanently warp our unborn future children with the staggering amount of venom I am about to steal from these kids so I can feel normal in this apartment.*

Back upstairs at Phoebe's, Peter and I smoked our secret cigarettes, buried ourselves into the couch, and watched a Monty Python marathon on cable until three in the morning. I even toyed with the idea of falling asleep—a revolutionary concept. Ever since I was a child attending slumber parties and sleepovers, I have always been the one to stay up the latest, whisper the longest, and giggle the loudest. I experienced a brief interruption in this tenure during high school when my mother was in charge of my curfew, but returned to form soon after—outlasting every party, every movie marathon, every last call. It wasn't that I necessarily even had to be having a good time; I was just in an endless *pursuit* of a good time. I was driven not by a zest for life but by an irrational fear—a fear of missing out. What if something wickedly funny happened just after I fell asleep? What if the next bar is insanely awesome? What if I leave and the next day everyone says, "You missed it. You had to be there"? What if my soul mate is about to walk into this party? What if Joss Whedon's car is about to break down in front of this party and he has to come in and drink scotch and regale us with tales of how the network screwed *Firefly*? How can I leave, go to bed, or otherwise end the night when the promise of something better, cooler, funnier, more amazing is just around the next dark and mysterious corner?

I had also spent years reinventing myself or, at least, desperately wanting to—a fear of missing out on hanging with the right crowd or being perceived as cool. As an elementary-schooler, I was a tomboy desperate to do all the things the guys did and therefore hid my ballet lessons from my peers. In middle school, I aimed for a walking Benetton ad look. By high school, I began to hungrily stare at the punk-rockers and alternative kids with their pocket chains, funky vests, pierced brows, and jagged haircuts—styles I was not allowed to leave my mother's house embracing. I remember wanting so badly to enter their world. But, as most people who have been through high school probably also later realized, the punks and skaters are every bit as elitist as the preppies in Limited Express sweaters and leggings—each crowd sneering at the other as though two fifteen-year-old girls from the same country, northeastern city, and high school actually had less in common than they shared. I would love to go tell those kids, *You think you don't have anything in common with me? Try going to Texas. Better yet, go abroad.* I thought the punky girls were more liberal and therefore more tolerant, but there is no tolerance for difference in high school no matter what side of the cool divide you're on. In college, I decided that clothes were poor markers of character; the cool-punk-chic look I had always dreamed of was just another uniform—a uniform of dissent. But college did not stop my lust for self-reinvention. I curated my taste in music, movies, and pop culture toward the crowd I was hanging out with—or the guy I was hanging out with—at any given moment. I could be a hippie, a hipster, or a geek all in one weekend. Like Play-Doh, you could shape me into any form and then ball me up and erase me—and then start all over again.

But the more I fell in love with drinking, the more I found the persona I had always been looking for: part Holly Golightly, part Dorothy Parker, with a dash of Sid Vicious thrown in for extra bad-assery. In my new guise, I didn't care much about conforming to other people's tastes because I didn't care much for people. And, as Holly-Parker-Vicious, I certainly wasn't going to bed early.

Who was I, after all, if not the sum of my experiences?

My worth was entirely calibrated by the exciting things I did, the wild places I went, the funny things I said, or the cultivated way I opined. Until sobriety, the idea that I was someone worthwhile and unique a priori had not occurred to me. And, as I looked toward the blank sober slate before me in the mirror, a thousand discarded personas on the floor, I began to sense that this one last transformation—that is, becoming myself, which is what everyone tells you to be from the start—was going to be an awful lot of fun. I was going to reinvent myself as me. And I could go to sleep as early as I damn wanted.

What a fucking relief. Going to bed when exhausted rather than pushing onward hoping for magic but ending up with a headache is truly empowering. I wish sometimes I could go back and tell a younger version of myself to leave a little mystery in her wake, tell her that the woman who leaves early—who doesn't absolutely *need* to be at given bar, party, or after-party—is far more thrilling than the one who is a constant, droning, and unavoidable presence.

But that New Year's Eve in 2009 with Peter in Phoebe's apartment, I didn't fall asleep while the party went on without me downstairs. I laughed with Peter and made him do his English accent and his British Muppet. He made us dessert. We made up jokes and stories about the film students. I chatted with friends every so often as they took breaks from the downstairs party. I lit more secret cigarettes, promised my-

self that this was a special-occasion vice, and snuggled into
the moment. Without intending to, I had stopped gritting my
way through the New Year; I had released the steely resolve
I thought I was going to need to make it through the night.
Unexpectedly—and isn't that always the way these things
come together?—I was having a pretty perfect New Year's
Eve: surrounded by happy friends (who were not limited by
my own psychotic needs), watching Monty Python, laughing with Peter, eating ice cream. And that's when I realized
that celebrating *every* holiday traditionally is overrated, that
dancing should be organic, and that Nick was right: No one
can dance to Led Zeppelin.

Number 9 on the Sacha Fantasy Relapse Pass: Back to Hunter

*I just cannot shake the image of my friend sipping
wine while Hunter S. Fucking Thompson hands her
a joint and continues to read from classic issues of* Rolling Stone. *It's still my favorite relapse fantasy—and my
only celebrity relapse fantasy. The truth is, there is no
one alive I want to lose my sobriety over. Who is there?
Amy Winehouse? We could spend the night shooting up
while she nursed a pet mouse and I slouched on her tan-
ning bed and waited for dawn. It just seems like a waste*

of a trip to London. Lindsay Lohan? We could drink vodka and Red Bull, dance until we sweated out our glitter body lotion, and then drive her Bentley into her beach house. I'm exhausted just thinking about that. While there are plenty of living artists I would love to meet, I cannot think of any with whom I would need to have an exotic chemical experience. Now, if Jack Kerouac passed me "tea" and whiskey at a jazz club, Truman Capote offered me a cocktail, or Dorothy Parker ordered a bottle and then asked what I was having—well, those are different stories altogether. Clearly, I've romanticized drinking with dead writers.

Still, even among dead writers, no one touches Thompson. In the 1960s and '70s, drug culture was the culture; the counterculture may have been counter but it was still a culture—and a big enough one to galvanize a nation of young people. We've since awoken hung over from that era's permissiveness as overdoses and AIDS came calling to crash the party. But, still, for a few years there, Drug Culture in all of its wayward romanticized glory existed. And had I lived then, my appetites—at least for a short while—might have been more, shall we say, appreciated. To have a few years of free love and drugs and rock and roll in a culture that made me feel good about it every step of the way—I'm not eroding brain cells; I'm expanding my mind, man—sounds pretty groovy to me.

Unwasted

And that's why my ultimate relapse fantasy is Hunter S. Thompson, circa 1970.

* * *

But these days, I am mostly out of the habit of thinking about the next raging party. When I watch a movie with lots of drugs and alcohol, I squirm. When I see friends drunk, I want to flee, not join in. These days, my fantasies are more likely to be about the single glass of wine with dinner, the cold beer on a hot day, the champagne flute raised in a toast. And, apparently, anything Hunter S. Thompson hands me. But there are no GET OUT OF JAIL FREE cards for this disease. There are no relapse passes, because once I take that drink, I don't know what's going to happen. Thompson's party, after all, ended with a gun in his mouth. And my experience tells me that, as soon as my brain gets a taste of that witch's brew, wires will crisscross, sanity will bend, and reason will wither. Experience tells me that sobriety isn't something I can slip in and out of without consequence.

So I have to ask myself, what am I willing to lose for this relapse? Am I willing to lose Peter? My job? The small world of good friends and neighbors I have created around me? My self-respect when I look in the mirror and realize I have to climb once more from the depths of addiction? Relapsing might come easy, but how many recoveries do

Sacha Z. Scoblic

I have in me? That's why I'm giving up on the "Top 10" relapse pass—even the time-traveling, body-swapping Hunter S. Thompson relapse fantasy. Because, when the weasels close in, I am way better equipped to handle them sober.

Chapter 10

Dry Run

A fter I'd been sober a year and the haze of recovery began to lift—that is, when I began to widen my daily travels to broader spheres than the short distance between the video store and my apartment—I noticed that, outside of B movies and puzzles, I had no appreciable interests at all. Years before, in graduate school, I had been forced to fill out a little get-to-know-you questionnaire to break the ice with my fellow students. Having no hobbies or any discernable extracurricular interests to speak of (save drinking, of course), I winged it—which is to say, I lied—and wrote: "skeet shooting" and "rapping on the mic." Imagine the disappointment of my classmates when they discovered I had neither a talent for weaponry nor hip-hop.

Since then, my extracurricular calendar had consisted solely of people instead of activities—who would I be meeting for drinks on what night. This, despite the fact that, over the years, I had signed up for and failed to attend classes in Bikram yoga, swing dance, Tae Kwon Do, and French cooking. And those were just the activities I lamely attempted and were nothing compared with my fantasy life, which included dreams of learning a foreign language, trying out for community theater, taking a pottery class, signing up for Smithsonian seminars, doing some volunteer work, forming a creative writing circle, visiting every museum in Washington, learning how to play an instrument (at one point the piano, at another the harp), freelancing for the local alternative weekly, becoming an active member of the National Zoo, joining a book club, and taking tennis lessons. And yet, about the only things I did with any regularity over the last decade had been watching movies and going to bars.

Now it struck me that I ought to do something about all those blank "About Me" boxes on every social-networking website I encountered, that I ought to capitalize on my newfound health. Because despite eating out every night and generally burnishing my form into the couch, I did feel like sobriety was indeed a newfound health. Naturally, I signed up to run the AIDS Marathon.

I found a brochure at my neighborhood Korean deli, So's Your Mom. ("So's Your Mom" always struck me as more of a playground retort than a deli name; I have always assumed the title is some odd Korean-to-English translation of "Just Like Mom Makes" or something.) Among the So's Your Mom community bulletin board ephemera were dog-walking services, meditation groups, bikes for sale, and a gold postcard with a seductive promise: "If you can run three miles, you can run a marathon." It was the National AIDS Marathon Training Program. I couldn't run three miles. And yet, in a kind of momentary insanity, I decided that hardly mattered. Neither did the fact that I had only recently quit smoking—again. I grabbed the gold postcard from the So's Your Mom bulletin board. It wasn't just impulsivity; it was a childhood dream.

When I was a kid, my Uncle Spencer, my father's older brother, had been an avid runner. Long before complicated health problems caught up with him, Spencer had been a kind of running icon in my life. In 1978, when I was five years old, my family and I traveled to Spencer's house in Brooklyn to watch him compete in the New York City Marathon. Spencer, his wife, Lorna, and their twin sons, Adam and Zac, my older and impossibly cool cousins, lived in a gorgeous brownstone in Park Slope that they had cleverly bought for a song well before that neighborhood had gentrified, let alone become the chic hub it is today. Visiting Brooklyn was always a treat for me. Whether it was the summer the twins got stilts and unicycles or the Christmas they tried to hypnotize everyone in the house ("This won't hurt a bit. You're getting very sleepy . . ."), Adam and Zac always seemed to be going through exotic phases I was too young to attempt or even to understand. They hung out in arcades and would take me to the subway station to point out the best graffiti. Eventually, as magic kits and crossbows yielded to punk rock and tattoos, the twins and their lives in Brooklyn just became cooler and cooler to the little cousin who came from a land made mostly out of shopping malls and snow.

I adored Spencer and Lorna as well—not least because they chose to make their lives in Brooklyn while my parents had stranded me in Syracuse. (As a child—and therefore not mindful of the vagaries of jobs and grown-up decisions—I always wondered why anyone would intentionally live in Syracuse; it was a matter I fully intended to rectify as an adult.) Spencer and Lorna also had the great sense to let their boys wear leather jackets and Converse All-Stars every day—traits I suspected were linked to their passion for New York City.

Back then Spencer had a shaggy, black beard and a long, lanky frame. Whether in jeans and sandals or his running gear, Spencer always exists in my imagination as eternally from the 1970s. He could look intimidating—until he laughed. Then his face seemed totally obscured by the beard, except for twinkling eyes, which were full of mischief. Also, Spencer loved *Doonesbury*, and I in turn loved him for being an adult who read cartoons.

And, of course, he ran. He ran every day. As young as five, I remember being jealous of that freedom. Spencer could just open the door, leave the house, and run—all by himself and whenever or wherever he wanted.

I remember snapshots of marathon day in New York City:

holding out water and feeling impossibly proud when one sweaty, thin runner grabbed the paper cup from my small hand. Watching Spencer round a corner in Central Park and my Aunt Lorna pointing, "There he is, sweetheart." And how fast that moment was over, how we had waited and how quickly Spencer had padded by. I remember runners who looked crooked and broken at the finish line. I remember wandering around Central Park in the sunshine while relatives tried to find the prearranged rendezvous point where Spencer would join us. Thousands roamed the park that day, but the special ones—the runners, the day's heroes—all stood out, wrapped as they were in silver foil space blankets like gods amongst us.

Later that night, Adam and Zac argued over which of the two of them would get to sleep underneath their dad's new space blanket. I understood intuitively that as a niece and not a son, I was not even in the running for the privilege of sleeping under the space blanket—but boy, did I want to. I wanted to feel that crinkly warm material around me, wanted to taste just a small moment of the accomplishment that went into earning it. For I saw it as a prize—one Spencer had selflessly given to his children—a special blanket to wrap around the special body that had run so far. Not realizing space blankets could be found cheaply anytime at the local camping-supplies store, I formed a plan. As Adam nestled into the silver blanket, setting off a round of crunchy noises and tiny arcs of light every time he shifted, and Zac glowered—occasionally reminding Adam that he, Zac, would get the blanket the next *two* nights in a row—I squirmed in my ordinary sleeping bag and plotted to run a marathon. I knew I would have to wait a very long time and that I would have to work very hard, but I would run a marathon, and I would get a space blanket of my very own.

And so, one Saturday morning in May of 2006, with my gold postcard from So's Your Mom in my sweatshirt pocket, I found myself standing with my new marathon training team in the shadow of our nation's Capitol. Stunned, I watched as people jogged, Rollerbladed, and biked around the National Mall as though it was some kind of giant playground—at 8 A.M. on a Saturday. What the hell were all of these people doing up at this hour? Saturday mornings were still kind of a mystery to me; for the past fifteen years, I had found them to be ideal for nothing more than sleeping. But now I saw there was life popping up all over the city. It was like the first time I went dancing at a gay club. *There are like sooo many gay guys here*, I thought. *Like a lot, a lot. Who knew?!* And it dawned on me that evening in the nightclub—Lizard Lounge or Badlands or Chaos, who can remember?—that there were entire worlds I knew nothing about. As I looked across our nation's manicured lawns, from the flag-footballers to the boot-campers, I realized I was discovering yet another new scene: Healthy People.

I was almost thirty-three, almost one year sober, and acutely conscious that it was now or never—or so I felt. Sobriety made me aware of all the time I had lost, and I felt old. The five-year-old me, who dreamt of space blankets and glory, had lost her way; she had ceded early-morning runs to sleeping off hangovers, had yielded her health to bottles and cigarettes, had relegated her enthusiasm for sports, for play, for daytime, and for life to nothing more than fantasy. Running was among those things I talked about doing rather than actually doing. I had led a vampire existence with no room for the wonder of little-girl dreams. But I was determined to resurrect those dreams; I owed it to the small five-year-old with space-blanket stars in her eyes. In that spirit, I had not run but loped, with dusty lungs and ice-pick cramps, through three miles of paved hell before being placed in a training group based on my time (such as it was).

There were few teams slower than us and what seemed like dozens of faster ones, including the herd we nicknamed the Gazelles, which appeared to be comprised entirely of supermodels and NBA All-Stars. It seemed they moved only in slow motion. They were constantly taking their shirts off to expose ripped, tanned abs on lean torsos as they stretched impossible limbs in a kind of soft-porn ballet. We, on the other hand, were the C students of the marathon, the Sweat-hogs. We had average bodies, bad knees, and at least a good decade between us and college. It seemed a tad ridiculous that each of our groups was reaching for the same goal. I eyed the Gazelles suspiciously as the coaches explained the task. To complete the mission at hand, we were asked to follow some simple rules: Run with the group every Saturday for ever-increasing distances and then run forty-five-minute maintenance runs just two more times each week.

Around this time, I noticed that maintaining my sobriety was starting to feel like its own marathon. I found myself bowing out of social events and even faking illness at the last minute. I thought marathon training might take my mind off of the sobriety that I was starting to earn One. Day. At. A. Fucking. Time. Replacing one marathon with another seemed only natural. Instead of continuing to hide from alcohol, I would run from it! Besides, I figured I had nothing to lose: The coaches told me, if I followed their rules, I would finish an epic race and experience incredible joy. I thought, worst case, I would descend into a dehydrated spider crawl, call it a day, go to rehab, and forget the whole enterprise.

I decided to act *as if* I could do it whether or not I believed I could. For a long time, that worked.

I did my two forty-five-minute maintenance runs twice a week and then joined my group in the inhuman predawn hours for long Saturday runs. We guzzled sports drinks the color of Windex and ate gumdrops made from salt. We were, among other things, a mortgage broker, a schoolteacher, a nonprofit administrator, a corporate consultant, and a scientist. Together we were friends. "Put a shirt on!" I would yell at a lithe, eight-foot-tall Gazelle in a bra top and athletic skort as she flew by us Sweathogs. "And eat a sandwich," added fellow Sweathog Lauren, the corporate consultant with an acid tongue. Meanwhile, Kasey, the scientist, and Nicole, the schoolteacher and our pace-group leader, would snicker as Thomas, the mortgage broker, would tell us to "Be nice, girls." But mostly we crammed those salty sport beans down our throats and discussed in precise detail all the food we would be eating when the run was over. It was a true ca-maraderie of athletes.

I set myself up for marathon success: I had a cohort of sup-porters; I followed the training rules (it didn't take long before I realized that skipping maintenance runs was an easy way to set my lungs on fire); I hydrated religiously after a bout of splitting headaches; I had my guilt-inducing Saturday morn-ing car pool in place, and I had faith in the coaches—like Todd, the cheeriest of the coaches, who would open Saturday runs with pep talks about how much we rocked his world. It was a delicately constructed house of cards designed to ensure success. And yet, when it came to sobriety, I resisted help at first: I resisted talk of higher powers, and I resisted the notion that a few simple rules and a cohort of support could be helpful. I was in control.

That's right about when I started to get very cocky about running, too. Maybe the training had just kick-started the latent runner in me. I started to have fantasies about the Iron Man triathlon (*I suppose I'll have to buy a bike*, I thought) and marathons around the world. I even imag-ined what it might be like to run with the Gazelles—the first five-foot-one-inch woman to make the cut. Who needed

213

support when you had the steely resolve of a champion coursing through your blood?

And then I ran twenty-three miles. I had already completed eighteen- and twenty-mile runs, accomplishments that had bolstered my confidence and secured my allegiance to the training program. But on the sixteenth mile of the twenty-three-mile run, I plummeted into crisis. I was suddenly and acutely aware of the seven miles between me and the end of the run—and that felt like a mind-numbing expanse. My legs were able, but my brain was seized with terror and my pulse echoed in my skull. I took uncomfortably shallow breaths and my heart fluttered; I wanted to wrest open my rib cage and let all the air outside in. Overwhelmed by the thought of continuing the run, but scared of quitting and watching my Sweathogs go on without me, I was in a panic.

How could this be happening? I mean, I was exercising! Shouldn't endorphins or some such be coursing through my body? Shouldn't my brain be bathed in serotonin right about now? And where was that runner's high I'd heard so much about? Instead of seeking support from the Sweathogs, I told them I was feeling tense but didn't elaborate; I didn't want to mess with their heads by explaining the whole seven-more-miles thing. I could tell that Thomas knew something was wrong, but he didn't push me; he just stayed by my side. "You're doing great," he said gently, as I quivered inside and looked up at him with frightened eyes. A giant part of me begged to stop; an equal force pleaded to go on.

I was trapped, and neither route led to relief. Split in two, I clenched my teeth and fists and barreled through. It was the first time since that initial white-knuckled three-mile lope that I had relied on willpower alone. It was no way to run.

There was no reprieve at the end of the twenty-three miles, just rage, tears, panic, and an uncontrollable urge to beat at the hollow, edgy sensation in my chest. I thought I would be unmasked, that Todd the coach would see I was not a runner but a crazy alcoholic person in high-end technical fabric. When I told Todd about my struggle on the course that day, however, he was unfazed. He explained that I was not stuck out there, that I had never been trapped. He gave me permission to take a break any time I wanted. He also gave me permission to fully confide in the Sweathogs (though I believe he said "teammates") without fear of sucking them into my madness. And if I kept running, he told me to remember that I chose to run. No one was forcing me to run. He had taken me this far, and now he asked me if I still trusted him. I did. "You had me at 'You choose to run,'" I said as I exhaled.

It began to dawn on me that perhaps I ought to reexamine my sobriety. Maybe I should choose to stay sober, not just accept it as my sad fate in life. Sobriety need not be an onus; it was, after all, the impetus to rediscover my childhood dreams. I would never have been able to train for a marathon while I was still drinking, if only because giving up my Friday nights for restful pre-run evenings would have been unthinkable. I began to wonder about all the goals that had been lost in drink, all the time I had wasted. How many books or articles did I never write because I decided to spend an evening drinking instead of writing (or, worse, drinking *and* writing only to find my prose turgid and inane in the cold hard light of day)? And how many dreams had I just plain forgotten all about? If sobriety was already helping to make one dream come true—the marathon—then maybe I shouldn't, heh, resent it so much.

When Spencer died, I was just twenty-three, the twins just twenty-eight. I was told a blood clot had blocked oxygen to Spencer's brain, and I raced to Florida, where Spencer had been living at the time. The twins looked shell-shocked, and I felt useless and in the way. Already a hard-partier, I had just returned to the States from a year abroad, during which time I had managed to drink my way through several Muslim countries. Still, I was at an age when I felt so vital, so unstoppable that I had no idea booze would ever limit me in any way. I was an adult, but a long way from grown up. Meanwhile, the twins were deep into their twenty-year-long Successful Filmmakers phase and casually telling stories about playing Boggle on set with the Beastie Boys. Honestly, trying to keep up with them is like trying to shoot laser beams out of your eyes using only your mind.

After Spencer's wake, my grandmother laid out a small collection of his personal effects: the tokens of a life now charged with meaning as my family and I gazed at trinkets from years spent in Ethiopia with the Peace Corps and in Romania on a Fulbright, papers written as a professor at New York University, dog-eared novels, and family photos.

What a big life he had, I realized. Somehow Spencer's firm place in my mind was as The Runner, but watching Adam and Zac gingerly touch dusty mementos, I saw how much more he was: a teacher, an expert, an adventurer. When asked if I would like something, I once more felt that odd tug of being the niece and not the son. Still, guiltily, I knew what I wanted. The space blanket was long gone, but I had had my eye on an old poster, crumbling at the edges; it was a photograph of the Brooklyn Bridge covered with thousands of people, and it read, THE NEW YORK CITY MARATHON 1978.

Spencer ran many marathons over the course of his life. And I don't know if 1978 was his first or just another along the way. I don't know why he kept that poster, if he cherished it or if he just simply never lost it. But 1978 was my first marathon and my fondest memory of Spencer. I carefully took the old poster home and had it mounted and framed, ripped edges and all. It has hung in every apartment I have lived in since then. At first, the poster was a keepsake of Spencer and a cute symbol of a longtime goal that, at twenty-three, I felt I would probably soon conquer. But as the years went on, the poster began to seem like a taunt, a nasty echo reminding me of all I was not accomplishing, of all the ways my life was not turning out as I had hoped, of all the ways I was letting myself down, of all the time I wasted.

When I started training for the marathon, Peter and I put

the poster at the foot of our bed, where I could look at it for inspiration before sleep as I readied for long Saturday runs. It has stayed there ever since.

Throughout that summer and fall in 2006, friends inevitably expressed admiration at my willpower to take on fifteen-plus miles at a time. And though I did not always disabuse people of this admiration, I knew a different truth: Willpower is what happens when you have to muscle through, but I didn't have to muscle through. I had an arsenal of support and ballasts in place to keep me on the right path. Those kooky coaches, like Todd—who yelled out cheesy and embarrassing cheers: "I see some heroes on the Mall today!"—were like hyper-euphoric angels, hell-bent on seeing us through the bizarre act of running exactly 26.2 miles. And when the road was really tough, the day particularly hot, and the edible runner's goo low, I would repeat, in a singsong whisper, *"I choose to run. I choose to run."* I'd look around at my sweet Sweathogs. *"I choose to run."* I'd stare down at my feet. *"I choose to run."* One in front of the other. *"I choose to run."* Sometimes, I'd look up to see I'd gone several miles in a kind of trance.

The day of the marathon was idyllic: not a cloud in the sky, 50 degrees, peak foliage; it was a perfect October day. Kasey had given me iron-on letters to attach to my AIDS Marathon tank top, which I had diligently affixed the night before. The childlike font spread across my sternum: *S-A-C-H-A*. The Sweathogs assembled that morning for the last time.

Nicole wore a tear-away warm-up outfit to keep her toasty while the rest of us hopped up and down, teeth chattering, our bare legs covered in goose bumps. A race photographer took our group's picture just before the marathon began. And then we were off, our *Iron Man* watches beeping in unison as we grinned at each other and kept saying, "We're doing it! We're doing it!" Less than two hours into the race, I saw Peter and my dad in Rock Creek Park. I wanted to stop and hug them, but I kept running, looking back and waving until I could no longer see them. The crowds cheered us on: "Go, Sacha! Yeah, Kasey!" Our lettered shirts had made us popular targets of support. I loved these strangers, these fans, these Washingtonians who on a beautiful day came out to watch the marathon—something I had not done since I was five years old, something I would have eschewed just a year before to nurse a hangover—and here I was *running* one.

As we ran onto the National Mall, the Sweathogs' training ground, I saw the Capitol before us, gleaming white as the red-gold trees arched overhead. My dad and Peter had taken the Metro across town and waited alongside the Mall; this time, I stopped to hug them. As the race stretched on, my group of Sweathogs diminished as some went ahead and others slowed. Ultimately, Kasey, Thomas, and I would stay together for the entire journey. We spoke about our season together, how perfect the day was, what we were doing after the race, which family members were in town to support us. But mostly I whispered, in rhythm with my feet, *"I choose to run.*

Sacha Z. Scoblic

I choose to run." And, when Thomas, beaming, said, "Proud of you girls," at mile twenty-five, I started to cry.

When I saw the end ahead of me, I screwed up my strength and sprinted as best I could, momentarily losing sight of the Sweathogs. I crossed the finish line and thought about Spencer padding by in Central Park and remembered him vividly walking toward us wrapped in foil like a knight back from battle, glorious, silver, sparkling. I thought, too, about my sobriety and all of the extraordinary things I might yet do. A marine put a medal around my neck and congratulated me; but I was looking for a different reward. "Space blanket?" I asked. He smiled and pointed to a box filled with camouflage-and-silver-foil blankets being swarmed by exhausted runners. But I was patient. I had waited decades; I could wait a few more minutes for the throng to dwindle.

By the time I wrapped the silver space blanket around my shoulders and collapsed into Peter's arms, I had found not only a new respect for my body, but a new respect for faith—a concept that would become integral to my recovery but one I had always disdained as illogical and submissive. I realized that I hadn't known everything, that the "possible" consisted of more than what I had experienced or conceived in my own head. My faith in Todd the coach, the Sweathogs, and the training program had opened me to having faith more broadly. Instead of muscling through all by myself, I yielded to advice, to support, and to the energy of a program that provided me with power and gave me more than

I could have ever received alone. After all, I would not have run a marathon if I had decided to train by myself. And so, I stopped seeing my sobriety as some kind of endurance test consuming every scrap of fight I had. Like marathon training, sobriety is not about willpower and white-knuckling it; it's about making the next right choice. I have since set myself up for sober success: I follow a few simple rules, go to twelve-step meetings, have faith in the guidance of others, let go, and surround myself with sober Sweathogs—the Wolf Pack.

Nowadays, I see my sobriety as a path I am running along; it is lined with people cheering for me. Sometimes I am running by myself, but sometimes I am running with Spencer, the Sweathogs, or with the Wolf Pack. And if I ever start to drift off the path—where the road gets sticky, where one is all alone, and where each step feels like moving through molasses—the crowd will smile and gently nudge me back to the center of the path. As I run along the sober path, nimbly and happily, I will pass milestones instead of mile markers, I will lose my fear, I will find my peace.

And sometimes, when even the sober path gets difficult and the road feels long, I will close my eyes and think, *I choose to run.*

Acknowledgments

Raise your sparkling ciders, and allow me to toast those who have been instrumental in helping me create *Unwasted*. My fantastic agent, Howard Yoon, patiently listened to my idea for a gimmicky nonalcoholic-drink recipe guide and then told me to go write a real book. Amy Pyle from Citadel got me and the book from the start and has been a truly insightful, funny, and encouraging editor throughout the process. Peter Catapano and Mark Lotto at The *New York Times* were early and ardent supporters of my addicted prose.

My deep appreciation to those great friends who are also talented writers and who read some or all of this book along the way, offering incredible advice, edits, and improvements: Jason Zengerle, Michelle Cottle, Lisa Gonzales, Kara Baskin, Steve Geng, and, especially, Amanda Fazzone and Ruth

Acknowledgments

Franklin (dear, dark, kind friend). Thanks also to Smith Glover, Stephen Masiclat, Adam Zimmerman, and Zac Zimmerman for their creative talents. I would also be remiss if I did not mention the friendship and support of Ivy Nitzkin, Amy Ressing, Amy Sullivan, and Noam Scheiber (who tried to stop the sinking ship). Thanks also to Stephen Stein for the mindfulness amid the madness. And to Bill W., Dr. Bob, and the Wolf Pack (you know who you are).

I have had the great fortune to work at the Aspen Institute while writing this book—an organization devoted to pursuing the big ideas. Walter Isaacson, who knows a thing or two about the importance of words, guides the Institute with boundless indefatigability, vision, and inspiration. It is telling that I started this project from this perch. I'd like in particular to raise my glass to my fearless captain, Jim Spiegelman, and my colleagues Jamie Miller, Jen Myers, Tarek Rizk, and the rest of the gang in our communications shop, all of whom supported my dream and carried the load when I left to write it. And a special thanks to Eric Motley and Dana Gioia, my in-house writing consiglieri.

My mother has endured years of insane behavior at the hands of her wild only child and should be sainted for time served. I hope to make her happy and proud as a gentler, more loving daughter nowadays. Her patience is exceeded only by her generosity of spirit. My sweet in-laws, Joseph and Barbara Scoblic, have never batted an eye at the odd and mouthy upstater at their son's side, and, for this, I am

Acknowledgments

especially grateful and charmed. Stephen Scoblic, thank you for being a brother, friend, and fellow traveler. Thanks to Dad and Deb for unyielding support, easy conversation, and a warm household that always feels like home. Dad, you are a quiet hero. And Shiloh, who makes my heart stop and head spin whenever I hear a magic word I never thought would belong to me: *sister.*

As long as there are days and nights to laugh and play and have adventures, then you will find me on J. Peter Scoblic's arm, grinning ear-to-ear. Peter makes all that is scary surmountable and all that is good transcendent. Without him, writing this book would quite simply have been impossible. With him, no moment is ever wasted.